Kay,
Thank you for [illegible]
and friend. [illegible] [illegible]
gary

I Am Here for You

Chaplain Gary Blaine

Kay Northcutt, Editor

Copyright 2018

Cover Photo by Wes McClellan

For Mimi and all of our children

In Memory of Vita Leo Brown

Many, many thanks to Shari Scheffler who was my proofreader and Chief Encouragement Officer.

CONTENTS

Introduction

Spiritual care means being fully present to the suffering of others and meeting them where they are without a whiff of judgment.

This book was cradled (held gently and protectively) in a weekly meditation that I emailed every Monday morning to the employees of the Susan B. Allen Memorial Hospital in El Dorado, Kansas. My reading audience included doctors, cooks, nurses, maintenance personnel, therapists, administrators, technicians, housekeeping services, medical coders, dishwashers, information technicians, and many more. I started writing to them and for them soon after I arrived, following a weekly habit I'd cultivated for 37 years in my work as a congregational pastor. I regularly wrote a pastoral letter to the people of my congregation, informative, sometimes downright educational, but hopefully also, *validating* and *inspiring* them as they went to their workplaces and schools and homes. Most of all it was a way I could be present to my congregation throughout their week. And so, as chaplain of the Susan B. Allen Memorial Hospital it seemed natural, in fact, to write a letter each Monday, not only informing them about the work of chaplaincy (what chaplaincy *is* along with what it is *not),* but also being *present* to them, by holding a mirror up to them—showing them what I *saw* them doing each day: their humanity; their redemptive, self-giving acts of care for their patients and for one another; and hopefully, to inspire them, as such work as theirs is exhausting, emptying and sometimes (many times) feels invisible. As chaplain I *see* them, and I *see* their work. I hold it up like the treasure it is—and inspire them to continue being who they are. My work is making visible and validating that which too often can be virtually unseen and fleeting. This is essential in a blue-collar oil town in central Kansas that is predominantly evangelical Christian. I am continually inspired by these people and hope to mirror back to them their own courage, compassion, and gentle humanity. Yet when I call them "ministering angels" they roll their eyes and dismiss me with "Oh, Chaplain." Candidly, my email to them was a way to be fully present to them, to their suffering, to walk side by side with them through the week.

I Am Here for You is not a book about how to do pastoral care. There are plenty of excellent resources for students and practitioners. Rather, I am writing about pastoral presence and pastoral relationships focused on hospital staff. Which is to say quite bluntly that I see myself not only as chaplain for those who visit our hospital as patients, but I see myself primarily as chaplain to the hospital staff. I am certainly not their chaplain because that is the title on my name badge! I became their pastor because I was there for the hospital staff of Susan B. Allen, from nurse to mechanic in every kind of crisis, whether it involves their patients, their co-workers, or their own personal needs. I have officiated at several of their weddings, baptized them (or their children), and have spent hours listening to them as they grieve a death in their family, fight depression, or cancer, or divorce. I dine with the employees in the cafeteria where we share stories about our families, horses, chickens and goats. We tell a lot of funny and sometimes raucous stories. *Very rarely* we discuss church or faith or the Bible.

My presence with these people and my abiding trust with them are reflected in a nurse who stops me in the hall and whispers to me, "Hey Chaplain, did you know I am pregnant?" Or, "Chaplain, I hope you will pray for my son. He is going to boot camp." Or, "Pastor, I think my daughter is doing drugs. What should I do?" And all too often, "Gary, I think my husband is having an affair and we are headed for divorce. Can I come and talk with you?"

I believe in these people, even the rakes and scoundrels among them. Despite all of their competencies and skills—which are daunting in scope and depth—they are easily devastated when a code goes from red to black. Our Family Birth Center can deliver a hundred healthy babies, but one neonatal death shatters them. At that point pastoral care is more than facilitating a debriefing session with them. It is loving them, affirming them, and encouraging them for months on end. Pastoral presence is honoring the limits of medicine and nursing, confessing the failures of people and processes, and absolving all with words of hope and forgiveness, abiding presence, and encouragement. Beyond all of the medical review procedures, medical ethics meetings, and the rewriting of protocols, pastoral presence is the dignity of bearing with these all too human beings and believing in them when all self-confidence has been eroded away.

How did I learn presence? Like many seminary students in the early 1970's I read Henri Nouwen's, *The Wounded Healer* and Brother Lawrence's *The Practice of the Presence of God. Diary of a Country Priest* by George Bernanos was also enlightening. But the authenticating presence that I spent decades learning came from my experience of suffering. I mean suffering in all of its manifestations, including that which was inflicted upon me, that which was self-generated, and that which I witnessed in the lives of others and for which I was and am impotent to ameliorate.

My first experience of suffering came at the hand of my father who was an angry and often violent man. He frequently whipped both my sister and me until we wore black and blue bruises—where they couldn't be seen: buttocks and upper legs.

The saving presence in my life was my grandfather, Herbert Pickett. We never talked about it but I knew he was deeply frustrated by my father's explosive rage. I spent most weekends at "Popeye's" house. We watched "Gunsmoke" on Friday evenings, spent Saturday mornings in his print shop, and went fishing in the afternoon. His gentle bearing, humor, and love of stories offered me an alternative insight to what it means to be a man. His presence was a safe harbor where I was deeply immersed in love.

The most embarrassing suffering is the self-inflicted type. It becomes embarrassing when you finally get enough sense into your thick head that your suffering reached out to hurt many others, like the spider veins in a window struck by a rock. The lines of pain extend beyond measure until the whole window collapses under the weight of disservation. My indiscretion in my first marriage not only brought divorce but also deeply wounded my children, parents and grandparents, parishioners, and friends.

But in the years that followed, most of the members of my family have graced me with forgiveness. My best friend, John Burciaga, took me out to lunch one day and made a statement I will never forget. He said, "Gary, you have been hurt and you have done some hurting, but you are still called to the ministry. It is time for you to return to your calling." It was the first word of grace I heard from any minister in nearly two years. We have stuck with each other for nearly thirty years. That is the kind of presence that psychotherapy could not tender me.

While I still bear guilt, I learned this about the course of suffering. It begins with attraction and flows to fantasy, to obsession, to planning, and finally to the actions that bring about suffering. I have learned how to recognize it, be present to it and patient with it until it has lost its strength. I can only sit with suffering if I understand her nature. It is also the path to grace. These lessons in suffering came to me most often from the Buddhist tradition, which still shapes my spiritual life.

And here's the miracle. Knowing all of this and the sordid details, Mimi Leo agreed to marry me.

Likewise, I have seen the same patient come into the emergency room dozens of times with the same diagnosis of diabetic ketoacidosis and testing positive for methamphetamine. Or consider the mother who is having a fourth baby. Her previous three children have been removed from her home because she is a drug addict. This new baby will also be removed because she tested positive for marijuana. The mother is beside herself with shock and sadness and protests, "This isn't fair." I also think of the COPD patient who is still smoking two packs of cigarettes a day. These are patterns of suffering that are self-inflicted.

As a parish minister I have served some wonderful congregations and social service institutions. They represent some of the finest people I have ever had the privilege of serving. And I have served some of the most dysfunctional and destructive congregations and organizations you could ever imagine. I have seen clergy and ministers of education or music lose their jobs because of inept and incompetent lay leadership. I have friends who have lost their positions under the scandal of rumor without the benefit of a hearing or investigation. I think the church is the last institution that still shoots its wounded.

What I have learned over four decades and offer to you is the chaplaincy of presence, especially when there are words that can neither explain nor console. I have learned to trust the gift of silence in the midst of exquisitely horrible, godforsaken suffering. And most importantly, I have learned to judge no one. I presume that every person has a song of sorrow and if I can be present to them they will sing it to me and perhaps we can discover wholeness together.

One of my favorite images from the Buddhist tradition is that of the lotus plant. The fleshy root tuber is planted in the mud. Stems rise up from the muck to make leaves and flowers. As we observe the gorgeous pink flower we forget all of the mud that sustained it in the first place. I am fully aware of the mud and compost that our lives are rooted in and I marvel at the blossoms that erupt on the surface of operating rooms, emergency rooms, rehabilitation services, and medical-surgical floors in acute stay hospitals.

Every week, indeed, every day at Susan B. Allen Memorial Hospital is a holy one. While none of us is a messiah, we all watch hope enter our doors in the expectation of healing and a fresh start in life. Sometimes we witness those hopes crushed. People die here. Lifestyles are often unalterably changed to something much less than the patient or family imagined. We also witness new sight for the blind, a mended arm or leg, and the fact that some rise up from their beds and walk out of here. Death and resurrection is our daily bread. We cannot be like the disciples of Jesus and run away from every trial, even the cross. We cannot hide from the stillborn baby, the end-stage cancer patient, the massive heart attack, or the loss of memory or sanity. Like the faithful women at the cross we tend to all who suffer, dress their wounds, work for their restoration, and trust that nothing can separate us from the love of God. And all of the time our feet are rooted in mud.

I am sharing this compilation of weekly writings with you in the hope that you too can find inspiration and comfort. Perhaps there are a few insights into human suffering and those who do battle with disease, trauma, and death. Despite everyone's best efforts, pastoral care is the end of the line in modern medicine. Spiritual care means to be fully present to the suffering of others and to meet them where they are without a whiff of judgment.

The value of spiritual presence became evident to me one day in the Emergency Room. I had been paged to trauma bay #6 for a code blue. CPR was in progress as the response team gathered.

The team included the ER doctor, nurses, technicians, and a PCC nurse who served as scribe. Lab technicians, diagnostic imaging technicians, and respiratory therapists were lining up in the hall. The patient's daughter was standing at the foot of the bed. Wearing a clerical collar I am easily identified as the chaplain.

She looked at me and said, "I don't want him in here."

In the midst of compressions, intubation, Foleys, and blood draws a nurse raised her head and said, "But I need him in here."

And so: I am here for you.

The Work of My Chaplaincy

1

This is not an educational book for students of pastoral and spiritual care. There are plenty of board certified educators out there who are better equipped than I. I cannot tell you "how to do" chaplaincy. My intent is to share with you the work and heart of my pastoral care and calling. Perhaps you can get a glimpse of that in this story with a patient named Jimmy.

At work I wear a clerical collar, Anglican style. The clerical collar is a quick and easy way for people to identify who I am. One day I was standing at the nurses' station in the Intensive Care Unit. I started to make my way into a room when the patient shouted out, "I just want you to know I am an atheist." I replied, "Not my problem," which stumped him but also made him chuckle. Over the next week I got to know Jimmy quite well.

When I met Jimmy he was morbidly obese, a noncompliant diabetic, a smoker with congestive heart failure, and he suffered from pancreatitis. He had a history of alcohol and prescription narcotic abuse. He hated the VA hospital system.

Jimmy loved his father. "He taught me how to hunt, fish, and play poker. We were like buddies and talked about everything." Jimmy's father died when the boy was sixteen. "I went to the funeral service in the Baptist church, and when I walked out of there I never went into a church again." He lived at home for two more years with an abusive mother who died at home of cancer. From there Jimmy joined the Air Force.

Jimmy had big dreams for his life. He imagined that he would serve his commitment to the Air Force (Vietnam era) in intelligence work. From there he would return to civilian life, find the girl of his dreams, get married, have children and grandchildren. After discharge he went to work for one of the aircraft companies in Wichita, got married, and had a daughter. Several years later he was divorced. His daughter had an automobile accident that made it impossible for her to get pregnant.

Jimmy's attitude was belligerent and angry, his behavior was self-destructive, and he was coping in the negative numbers. This assessment did not require rocket science. Jimmy would have flat out refused to engage in a palliative care plan that would encourage him to establish health goals. He was very intent on killing himself.

But there are subtleties in the soul of this man that do not point to a crisp intervention strategy.

In terms of attitude Jimmy would be easy to write off if he was indifferent. But Jimmy was angry which led me to think that he had dreams and plans that continued to have merit in his mind and sense of self. He had not done the grief work that he needed to do since adolescence. The loss of his marriage and hope for grandchildren added layers of remorse over the soul of a child who lost his hunting buddy. In the little time I had to work with Jimmy I would try to unpack the losses, encouraging him to tell the stories of his father and how they point to his sense of self.

I also wonder if all of the losses that Jimmy experienced gave him the message that he did not merit the fulfillment of his dreams. Does he imagine that he only deserved to get fat, sick and die without progeny? And in that frame of mind wouldn't it only make sense that the same God who took his father lorded over the shipwreck of his life? Jimmy's issue with God is not God's absence but God's abandonment of him right in the heart of adolescent personality development. His spiritual suffering continues to feed his depression.

His behavior also points to the last conclusion. Why not destroy the only thing he has left, his body? He at least could be in control of that. Until Jimmy sees the relationship between his losses and his behavior there is little hope of healthy coping and wholeness.

Jimmy was not really an atheist. He was too angry with God to deny God's existence. In my last conversation with him I said, "You may not believe in God Jimmy, but I know something else about you."

"What's that?" he snarled.

"You are a man of conscience. If you weren't none of this would matter to you."

There was a long pause and he mumbled, "Just don't tell anybody."

That afternoon Jimmy was transferred to the VA hospital in Wichita. I have never seen him since. I do not know if this pastoral care assessment guided him to healthier outcomes. I could only meet him where he was. There was no great revelation or transformation, and certainly no conversion. Our relationship was an authentic one as far as it went. Jimmy's story was told and he was received with abiding presence and deep listening.

Today's standards of pastoral care require an outcomes focused care plan. It is an important and worthy goal, but one that greatly depends on a patient who has some hidden source of strength and grace that will sustain them through their disease. I cannot give that to them. This kind of work is also greatly crippled by the fact that ours is an acute stay hospital that works primarily to get people past the crisis stage of their healthcare needs. They may be with us for one to five days. From there they will go back to their primary care physicians, outpatient therapy, home health, nursing homes, residential rehabilitation facilities, and local congregations for spiritual nurturance, if they have one.

Before venturing into the ways and means of my chaplaincy I would like to offer something of my credo. You have already seen that I use terms like "live and move and have our being in God," or refer to God as "Creator, Sustainer, and Redeemer." These are formulaic and traditional uses of Christian talk, but I fear you will only hear them as such. I use them partly because that is the language of the people I work with. But there is a deeper meaning in my own soul that gives me the foundation for my work.

Any god that can be defined is not a god worth worshipping. Please do not ask me to define what I mean by God. There is nothing more troubling than personal orthodoxy. Belief has little value to me if you define faith as right belief. Right belief is ephemeral and fleeting. It is like thinking that the chatter that is going on in your head is who you really are.

I have experienced the Sacred, the *Élan Vital,* that impetus for creating and creative life. At every moment God transfuses and transforms all the nations, peoples, and creatures of this planet and universe. All of creation is and exists within the Holy One. I have had no experience of God beyond this life, this earth, these peoples, minerals, plants, and animals. Pierre Teihard de Chardin put it this way, "By means of all created things, without exception, the divine assails us, and molds us. We imagined the divine as distant and inaccessible, when in fact we live steeped in its burning layers."

I have learned that I cannot experience God only with the

good stuff like hiking the Appalachian Trail, watching the birth of my children, or spending a week with Thich Nhat Hanh. I have learned to open myself to the presence of God, or the Force, or the Source in the midst of baptizing a stillborn infant, clawing my way through a divorce, and watching us destroy this planet. God is the passageway of both birth and death and all of the joy and tragedy of being human. I have wept through the painful mistakes I have watched my children make and wept with joy at their triumphs. It is all sacred stuff. God does not get any closer to us than that. I think the psalmist said something about God knowing our coming in and going out.

Am I saying that God causes us to suffer and participates in creating war and environmental destruction, and natural disasters like hurricane Katrina? Life happens, disease happens, age happens, and death happens. As Jesus mentioned, there are wars and rumors of wars and so on. I do not believe that God is the "first Cause" of Creation and all that unfolds within her, certainly not in the literal sense of that idea. If I believed that I would have to confirm to my patients and their families that, yes, God is the cause of your diabetes, Parkinson's disease, and the fact that you were T-boned in an intersection because you ran a red light.

I believe that God is the Beginning and that has to include the waters of chaos and the power of the Holy Spirit to move the seas of death to make room for life. Creation is ever a process of evolving and dying and rising again. I see this Sacred Power everyday in my chaplaincy. Proud parents show me the sonogram of their first baby and I hold hands with a man in his fifties who is dying of cancer. I watch alcoholics who are vomiting blood and agonizing in the pain of cirrhosis of the liver leave the hospital. The first stop on their way home is the liquor store; all of this in the presence of God. God is in the joy of those young parents and the suffering of that alcoholic. I am learning with St. John of the Cross:

"What is grace?" I asked.

And he said, "All that happens."

Let me tell you about the last time I saw Mary Jane Ware. I knew Mary Jane for about three years, and met her on and off in our Cancer Center or as an inpatient. On her final discharge she was sitting in a wheelchair in the lobby of the hospital, waiting for her ride home. I stopped to talk with her, bending over to hold her hands. We said very little, but held each other in our shared gaze for several minutes. Her grip was firm and she held me tightly. I asked, "Mary Jane, is there anything else I can do for you?"

"No," she said. "I am just appreciating the moment."

God is that moment. We knew that this would be the last time we would ever see each other again. It was a vision of deep human dignity and heart felt gratitude.

My experience with people is quite similar. I am often left in awe when I watch doctors and nurses treat patients who are screaming in pain, excreting fecal matter out of their mouths, and managing a methamphetamine overdose patient who is as paranoid as a cat in a washing machine. People can be noble, courageous, and dignified in the most terrifying circumstances. I expect this of people. And, I also expect them to screw things up. Mistakes are made, biology works against us, and we sometimes do things in anger and spite. We can be creative and self-destructive in the same hour.

This is the faith canvas from which I work.

The place where I work is the Susan B. Allen Memorial Hospital in El Dorado, Kansas. El Dorado is an oil town and the refinery is the largest employer in the city. A state correctional facility is there, along with the county seat, schools, churches, and businesses. Oil fields and cattle ranches, row crops of milo, corn, soybeans, and wheat surround it.

The hospital is a 70-bed acute stay hospital. Susan B. Allen hosts a cancer treatment center and dialysis center. There are nearly 400 employees. Every Monday morning I write the "Chaplain's Chart." Each entry is meant to educate, inspire, encourage, and celebrate the hospital staff. The "Chaplain's Chart" entries that follow were designed to educate hospital employees about the work of chaplaincy.

*****

6

What Is a Chaplain Anyway?

As a hospital chaplain I never dare presume what a person's faith is or what it means to them, or what it should be. Nor do I know their relationship with God. Such presumption is a dangerous and even sinful judgment to make. Because I cannot know, and dare not presume, I am never in the position to critique their faith with God. This is not just a matter of professional values on my part, but a deep conviction that when Jesus said we are not to judge others he meant all others – no exceptions. This is a fundamental perspective that I have toward each of you, our patients, and their families.

I have learned through many years of experience that those who are the most judgmental are the most insecure in their faith. If someone does not have the same faith that they have, such persons must not be "saved" and are therefore "damned." These people tend to view God as angry, wrathful, judging and punishing. They have what is called a "paranoid worldview" that is distrustful and suspicious. I am never surprised to learn that these same people had parents who were angry, wrathful, judging and punishing. Or, they have a troubled past that may have included some form of addiction such as alcohol, substance abuse, or sexual addictions. Others have done some things that hurt a lot of people, especially in their family, and they are terribly burdened by such guilt that they believe that they and others are only worthy of punishment.

Paul declared, "All have sinned and fall short of the glory of God." (Romans 3:23) Notice that the word "fall" is present tense, suggesting that none of us have ever fully become the blessing that God created us to be. Paul goes on to say that does not matter anymore. The love of God is greater than our sin, past and present. He claims that the power of sin and death is broken in the crucifixion and resurrection of Immanuel. Immanuel is the name given to Jesus, meaning "God with us." To put it another way, God gave God's self to be with us, even so far as to submit God's self to the violent power of the Roman Empire, represented by the cross. This is the radical gospel of the Christian religion. Most of the ancient world thought that people made sacrifices to their god in order to satisfy or appease that god. The Christian faith turns this on its head. God can only do what humans can never accomplish – give God's self for the restoration of the world.

People often ask me if I "save souls." The answer is no. Only God can bring salvation and as I have already suggested, that work is done, salvation is complete. Because I believe that this is true there is no need for me to judge others, or worry about whether or not they are going to be saved and go to heaven. God is always Immanuel – God is always with us. My ministry is to share that sacrificial love in the hope that comfort is brought to others. My calling is to share that "Good News." In the words attributed to St. Francis of Assisi, "Preach the gospel at all times and when necessary use words." Through presence and prayer, deep listening and discernment I hope to be a witness to the grace I can never give to others.

This may be more of a faith statement from me than you ever wanted to read. Not everyone shares my theology. I just wanted you to have some sense of the faith that I bring as a Chaplain. And don't believe for a moment that these pages contain the deep mystery that is my faith in God. I do hope that you know that I respect you, wherever you are on your faith journey. That is why I can honestly say that I am here for you.

The Blessing of Powerlessness

Father Brennan Manning is well known for his books such as *The Ragamuffin Gospel, Abba's Child,* and *All is Grace.* His spiritual director was Larry Hine who offered him this blessing:

> May all of your expectations be frustrated,
> May all of your plans be thwarted,
> May all of your desires be withered into nothingness,
> That you may experience the powerlessness of a child
> And can sing and dance in the love of God
> The Father, Son, and Holy Spirit.[1]

At first glance that seems like a very negative thing to say

The Christian Century, April 16, 2014, Vol. 131, No. 8, p. 9.

8

to a young priest at the beginning of his ministry. Yet I cannot deny that in 41 years of parish ministry many of my expectations have been frustrated, plans thwarted, and desires withered. This is the dying to self that we must all experience if we are ever to know and appreciate the powerlessness of a child who can sing and dance in the love of God. That is what we are created for and our expectations, plans, and desires must be washed away if God is to ever shape us for singing and dancing.

What does it mean to sing and dance? I think it means that with our self out of the way we are free to serve the needs of other human beings. When we are no longer preoccupied with defending our ego and satisfying our hungers we can defend the poor, feed the hungry, and heal the sick. Pride does not allow us to scoop up a crying child or mentally ill person and hold them against the breast of compassion. Fear does not allow us to take a street person home to bathe, feed, or clothe. We can only give ourselves to others when we set aside our expectations, plans, and desires.

Very simply, I think this is what Holy Week is about. The cross was the symbol of the power of Rome. It was prominently displayed and used to keep people in their place. Under the Roman Empire the cross was the sign of death in a culture of imperial occupation and dominance. The Christian witness is that Jesus marched up to Golgotha, took his place on the cross and turned it into a symbol of life and resurrection. He transformed a major emblem of the state's deathly power into one of love and hope. But he could only do that by the willing sacrifice of his own life.

I see this same sacrifice throughout the hospital. You may think you are just doing your job: cleansing a wound, changing the diaper of an incontinent elder, encouraging a new mother, easing the pain and fear of a cardiac patient. You may think of these as "protocols" or bedside manner. I think of it as ministry. And the best of us are the ones who have learned to let go of the self, wave goodbye to frustrated expectations, bless the thwarted plans and withered desires.

However you celebrate the week I wish you all the blessing of God and life.

Listening to the Stories of Others

A chaplain's first responsibility is to listen to the stories others tell about their lives. We tell stories to talk about what has happened or is happening to us. For example, when I call on someone who has just had an accident or whose loved one has died, they need to tell me what happened. Sometimes they need to tell the story several times so that their mind can put its arms around events and how those events are changing their lives. Maya Angelou said, "There is no greater agony than bearing an untold story inside you." Once the story is told people can begin to interpret the story and to think about how their identity has changed with the death of a loved one, a newborn baby, or a diagnosis of prostate cancer. Only then can they imagine the next step in their lives. That is how a new future begins to open up for us.

When might someone need the chaplain to come around and hear their story, or better yet, to swap stories with? Here is a brief list: the death of a loved one, career changes or loss, family conflict, tough ethical decisions, anxiety or depression, spiritual conflict, and bereavement. And by the way, sometimes it is just as important to get together and tell the funniest joke we ever heard!

Rituals and symbols play a big part in story telling. These are gestures and images that convey a meaning that interprets and transforms the story to deeper mystery. For example, when we read or tell the story of Betsy Ross we often see her sitting in a rocking chair with Old Glory on her lap as she finishes sewing the thirteenth star on the field of blue. The image of the flag on her lap reveals a well of history, struggle, and aspiration for human freedom. Likewise, as a chaplain, I offer a rich array of symbols and gestures to transform the human stories of struggle, triumph, despair, joy, death and hope. These stories are told every day at our hospital. And to those stories I can bring baptism to one who is dying or stillborn, anointing to one who is sick or dying, Holy Communion, marriage, or the joy of a daily blessing. All of these are times when you or our patients can use me.

Stories, rituals, blessings, and symbols are the basic tools in my chaplain's kit. Each is a means toward wholeness.

So I send to you this slender cord in the hope that our love and faith can thread the deep.

I am here for you, and I would love to sit down with you and hear your story.

Groping or Sacred Touch

For the past few weeks the lead stories on national news have been this, that, or another public figure who is accused of sexual harassment or assault or rape. It is a sad commentary on our ethical norms as a nation. One would have hoped that we had moved a little further down the moral path than fondling a woman's breast or genitals and bragging about it. And the arrogance of answering the doorbell in nothing but a bath towel is really rather pathetic. It isn't just the contempt that assaults women, it is the arrogance that a guy has just the body that every woman wants to see.

I remember when charges of pedophilia amongst Roman Catholic clergy began to gain public notice in 1984. It soon mushroomed into a major public scandal that is not over yet. It has cost the Church over 4 billion dollars to date. I had a very dear friend in Father Marty. He was past the age of retirement but the diocese was so short of priests they kept him on as long as possible. One day at lunch, Marty told me, "I feel like I am carrying the casket of the church with me every place I go."

In the denominations that I have served, mandatory sexual harassment training continues to this day. Initially the lesson I learned was "touch no one." I always asked my church secretary to stay behind if a female parishioner had requested a late afternoon or early evening appointment. I kept my office door open. I do not go to the home of a female parishioner alone. I never hold or touch children unless I am in a very public place. I have windows installed in my office doors, even here in the hospital.

And you know what? That is also rather pathetic.

I have had to relearn the value of the human touch. Eye contact and touching are sacred vessels in hospital chaplaincy. Holding hands, hugging, and making the sign of the cross on a dying one's forehead are holy gestures that convey grace that words alone cannot communicate. Holding the body of a deceased fetus and singing to him, "This Little Light of Mine," is my sacred office. There are times when I hug a parishioner, or patient, or employee, knowing it is the only human touch they will receive all week. Some people give me a hug as if they are hanging on for dear life.

Sacred touching, even as simple as a pat on the back, is ritual with the power of blessing. It means you are loved beyond your qualifications for being a lovely person. You are embraced when all others would flee from you. You are blessed, not so much as by this chaplain, but by the very love of God. I just happen to be the available arms and hands of God.

I believe this is the kind of touching the world is desperate for. We have had too much groping, too much hitting, too much spanking and slapping. We yearn for the gentle touch of God's mercy with no other agenda than kindness. And I dare say, even sex offenders yearn for the hand of God when all the world would hang them by their gonads.

This is what I have learned over the past thirty years and what I am ready to risk. I make no excuses for predators, but neither will I deny the kiss of grace. I, like every other human being, have fallen short of the glory of God, and I am blessed that God's fingers have swooped me up when all others were scolding.

A Purveyor of Hope

As a clergyman I am a purveyor of hope in a culture of commercial fear. The setting of ministry does not matter, be it the parish, social justice ministry, industry, or clinical chaplaincy. I understand fear to be quite different from anxiety. Anxiety is the general and often subtle feeling that things are not quite right, our future is uncertain, and we are not confident that we can meet the future with skill and competence. Fear is the perception that our lives are in danger or somehow threatened. Fear can be the verifiable fact that we are about to be consumed by a lion – or cancer. Granted, fear can also be a matter of perception that we are in immediate peril. Real or perceived, fear often causes us physical, emotional, and spiritual anguish.

Fear is a biological reaction. When the human brain perceives a threat sympathetic nerve fibers of the autonomic nervous system are activated and hormones are released that prepare us for what is generally called the fight or flight response. Some people are frozen into inaction. The physical symptoms include increased heart rate and blood pressure, perspiration, acute sensitivity, and aggression. I have heard a family member say to someone in acute distress, "get a grip," or "man up." I understand that we get embarrassed when a loved one seems out of control, but it is not possible for them to override the biological response to fear and magically regain control.

Fear is emotional. In the fight or flight response we are no longer able to reason. We cannot calmly sit back and evaluate the threat, consider the reasonable courses of action, and make a rational choice on the statistical data that would guide a decision. When we are frightened most of us tend to be very defensive, untrusting, and will lash out verbally and physically at the very people who are trying to help. The comment "get a hold of your self" or "grow up" or "quit feeling sorry for yourself" does not usually work because the person's biological and emotional systems are overloaded with pain and stress, and those hormones that prepare us for the fight of our lives.

Fear is spiritual. One of the many understandings of spirituality that I use as a chaplain is the power of meaning and purpose. In acute and chronic disease or trauma, pain and disability radically challenge the meaning and purpose of our lives. We are less than honest with ourselves when we deny the impact of a disease like diabetes, or the loss of a loved one, or a permanent disability on our sense of identity and purpose. Somehow "have faith" just doesn't cut it.

The Buddhist teacher, Pema Chodron, wrote that, "Fear is the natural reaction to moving closer to the truth." And there is nothing like a stroke, or shattered leg, or a miscarriage to move you closer to the truth. I mean the truth that asserts our limitations and mortality, and crushes the illusion that our lives are immune from disease and death.

The psalmist declared, "Even though I walk through the darkest valley, I will fear no evil, for you are with me, your rod and your staff – they comfort me." (23:4). Though God walks with us we still have to enter the darkest valley. Faith is not a "get out of jail free" card. Every human being has to walk through the valley, some through many valleys. The hope the psalmist offers is that the Creator of life is with us, even when we have our backs against the wall, we are frightened out of our minds, and faith is a waning thing. Sometimes the real faith work begins after the crisis is over and we are given time to renew our trust in the powers of life that has brought us this far and the certainty that life is both precious and vulnerable.

I am here for you, even if it only means holding hands and walking through valleys.

Keeping My Finger on the Pulse

What is the role of the chaplain? Generally, I see my role as a welcoming and non-anxious presence to everyone who enters this building. This includes patients, their families, medical personnel, and all of those essential folks who care for the building, prepare our food, and clean patient rooms and our offices. Regardless of our faith tradition, each of us is charged with compassionate caregiving. I am also given the labor of a Sacred Presence, the Spirit of Life in whom we live and move and have our being. From birthing to dying (and sometimes that can be the same event) God is with us and part of my job is to keep my finger on the holy pulse of life.

Remember that fear is biological, emotional, and spiritual. The ancient Greeks used the term "psyche" to refer to the human soul. That is where we get the word "psychology." For the Greeks, however, psyche was not limited to the emotions. They understood that the human soul was an all-inclusive term that meant the rational mind, the depths of emotions, the imagination, and will. The Greeks had a systemic understanding of the human mind/soul and knew that we really cannot understand a person until we can see all of the parts working together. They are dynamic and wisdom dictates that we understand and care for them all. One of the strengths of our

14

hospital is the general orientation that we treat the whole person.

My prayer every morning is that I see the face of God in every person I meet. What they believe or their religious affiliation – even if they have none – is not the point here. In fact, these people teach me more about the Sacred than I ever imagined before. How does this happen?

I try very hard to listen. I want to hear their story, the journey that brought them to this place, where they think their future path lies and how they will get there. I want to discern their hopes and fears, their strengths and limitations, and the spiritual resources of meaning and purpose that will see them into that future. If a pastoral prayer is appropriate, that prayer will reframe what I have heard and invite the unconditional love of God to meet these very human needs. Sometimes those needs include comfort, courage, hope, acceptance, and trust. Sometimes those needs reflect a concern for a loved one at home, unfinished work in field or office, or who is caring for the family dog. And there are times when pastoral care means that I engage conversations about end of life care, durable power of medical attorney, living wills, and DNRs. Always I give thanks for the work that you do, celebrating the skills of doctors, nurses, and technicians.

Sometimes silence is the best prayer, as attested to by this unknown author:

> With silence only as their benediction,
> God's angels come;
> Where in the shadow of great affliction
> The soul sits dumb.

By dumb the author does not mean stupid, but rather, quiet and still.

I will be quiet now and move onto the floors of the hospital. I will continue to write about my work with you in the hope that the role of the chaplain can be a part of this wonderful team. In the meantime, go in peace.

Serving the Perfectly Dreadful Person

My tenth grade English teacher introduced me to this short little poem by Edwin Markham. It is one that I have used ever since. I am sure you have heard it.

> He drew a circle to shut me out;
> Heretic, rebel, a thing to flout.
> But love and I had the wit to win,
> We drew a circle that took him in.

Regardless of the reason why, we are often met by people who try to draw circles of exclusion. Typical excuses are race, religion, nationality, ethnicity, gender, ability, age, gender identification, and political affinity. We meet a lot of prejudiced and hateful people every day in our lives. They are always trying to shut us out, cut us off, disrespect and disregard us. Add pain, suffering, and the fear of death to their native biases and they can be perfectly dreadful people to serve or serve with.

Sometimes we meet patients and their families who will not hear anything that we might offer them in terms of medical or nursing treatment, therapy, or end of life care. By their actions we learn that they are not only noncompliant but down right self-destructive. It is very tempting to write them off. Too often we make dismissive comments about them and the level of our care begins to wane.

We cannot stop people from drawing circles of exclusion. We just need to keep a good supply of chalk, crayons, and marking pens in our pockets to draw wider circles of love and wit. If they continue to shut us out then we just draw a wider circle – and another – and another, as long as they are in our care.

You see, the point here is not their circles of prohibition, but our circles of compassion, knowledge, and wisdom. They may proscribe every therapeutic intervention that we carefully build for them. But we cannot let their fearful interdictions countermand our professional responsibilities. We offer to the best of our ability the highest quality medical and therapeutic protocols and procedures that we know of. As autonomous persons they have every right to reject them. As professionals we have every responsibility to offer them continuous care.

When we find ourselves drawing lines and not circles we need to take an inventory of our own ego, with a heart full of anger, fear of failure, or the anxiety of being rejected. These are the times when I repair to the great circling prayer of St. Francis of Assisi. It is a powerful prayer when you have to draw a lot of circles.

> Lord, make me an instrument of thy peace,
> Where there is hatred, let me sow love;
> Where there is injury, pardon;
> Where there is doubt, faith;
> Where there is despair, hope;
> Where there is darkness, light;
> Where there is sadness, joy.
> O Divine Master, grant that
> I may not so much seek
> To be consoled, as to console;
> Not so much to be understood, as
> To understand; not so much to be
> Loved as to love;
> For it is in giving that we receive;
> It is in pardoning that we are pardoned;
> It is in dying that we awaken to eternal life.

Please know that you are all welcome into my circle.

Tell Me Again, What is a Chaplain?

Probably the image of the chaplain's work that first comes to mind is the care and consolation of patients. The image is that of the chaplain holding hands with a patient, praying with them, or sitting in a dim room awaiting the courser of death. The image can shift to a quiet conversation in a hallway with a staff member, greeting someone in the emergency department's waiting room, and stopping by the chair of a dialysis patient. The scene can expand to gathering

17

with a family to discern the need for hospice care or memorial services.

We seldom imagine the broader context of the institution. The fact of the matter is that pastoral care is anemic if it is only understood as a matter of private faith by the chaplain or the hospital. Pastoral care is as social as it is individual. Or to put it another way, pastoral care is about the whole system, not its unique and separate parts. Therefore, it matters to me as the chaplain how we work together, how we communicate with each other, how we manage tension or conflict. Part of my responsibility as chaplain is to keep my eyes and ears open to morale, camaraderie, and the processes of teamwork.

Perhaps you remember this bit of wisdom from an unknown author:

> For the want of a nail the shoe was lost.
> For the want of a shoe the horse was lost.
> For the want of a horse the knight was lost.
> For the want of a knight the battle was lost.
> For the want of the battle the war was lost.
> For the want of the war the country was lost.

Chaplains listen for the ping of nails falling out of horseshoes. And when I hear that sound, I start asking questions like:

- ➢ I wonder if we could talk about what happened?
- ➢ What is the process by which we review our team responses?
- ➢ Who is it that you need to be talking to besides the chaplain?
- ➢ What is to be learned from what happened and how we approached it?
- ➢ I wonder why people seem so tired or melancholy or frustrated today?

Some might find these questions irritating but I can roll with that. The questions are not meant to blame anyone. Remember the issue is the system, the team, the department, and the hospital. Personally we are only as effective as the rest of the team. From nails to nations we have to look at the whole organism. When we think this way we realize that the farrier is as important as the king.

When we fail to think about the organic nature of our work together we find ourselves feeling unsupported and undermined; and that is when we start pointing fingers and gossiping about others. Isolation is the first step to burnout.

These words may not seem "spiritual" or even "inspiring." But I love you enough to tell you that they are at the heart of community life that we call family, team, department, and hospital. The beloved community is the context of faith, hope, love, and healing.

I often find myself repeating Reinhold Niebuhr's "Serenity Prayer." *God grant me the serenity to accept the things I cannot change; courage to change the things I can; and wisdom to know the difference.*

Take heart for the snow is melting, seeds are watered, and the sun will warm the soil for new life. All of these parts will come together and present us with Spring.

The Sacrament of Pastoral Care

Pastoral care has a sacramental role that most people do not know about or see. The word "sacrament" generally refers to that which is sacred or holds a significant meaning. More specifically sacraments are the rites or rituals that symbolize the means of grace. In the Christian religion these are understood to be those rituals that were instituted by Jesus Christ as vehicles of grace. They celebrate the embrace of God's love. The two that are universally recognized are Holy Communion and Baptism, though these are not without their controversy in the history of the church. Other communions, such as the Roman Catholic Church, offer the sacraments of Reconciliation (also known as Penance), Confirmation, Marriage, Holy Orders (ordination), and the Anointing of the Sick, formerly known as Last Rites or Extreme Unction. Protestants may do all of these rituals but do not consider them "sacraments" in a formal way but "sacramental." Confusing, isn't it?

The sacraments that are most frequently celebrated here are Anointing, Holy Communion, and Baptism. On very rare occasions all three may be administered at the same time. I have a portable communion set that I can take to patient rooms. Patients or their families have asked to receive Holy Communion, and there is a brief liturgy for that sacrament.

The Anointing of the Sick may or may not suggest that death is immediate, but is a sign of blessing and the hope for healing. The anointing of oil is an ancient tradition that one can read about in many places in the Hebrew Bible. The 23rd Psalm declares, "You anoint my head with oil, my cup runs over." The anointing oil that I use is made of frankincense and myrrh, gifts of the Magi to the infant Jesus. One anointing prayer reads, in part, "As you are outwardly anointed with the holy oil, so may our heavenly Father grant you the inward anointing of the Holy Spirit. Of his great mercy, may he forgive you your sins, release you from suffering, and restore you to wholeness and strength."

We have had baptismal kits in the hospital for several years and we are now in the process of refurbishing them. Our friends in the maintenance department are making new boxes for them. One will be kept in the Emergency Department, and the other on the Family Birthing Center. The kits include bowl, towel, anointing oil, baptismal candles (not lit but given to the family for the celebration of "remembrance" on the anniversary of the baptism), baptismal certificates, and *The Book of Common Prayer*. The prayer book contains liturgies for all of the sacraments, prayers for the sick and dying, and the Psalter. Our volunteer chaplains are welcome to bring their own liturgical resources.

More often than not the baptismal kits will be used in the case of a stillborn or death of an infant. There have been occasions when adults have requested baptism. I am certainly willing to offer baptism in these circumstances but I know that some clergy will not because of their denomination's doctrinal beliefs. We have a list of local clergy who are willing to serve these people if I am not available. Baptism is also offered at the request of the mother or family.

In these situations theological debate about baptism becomes irrelevant. Baptism is the embrace of God's love and I cannot think of a time when we more desperately need that love than at the death of an infant or child. As Chaplain Wesley Don Cohoon wrote, "An infant who dies will never have an opportunity to profess his/her faith or experience many life events. Therefore baptizing the baby may be the family and baby's only opportunity to celebrate God's grace on this earth." Baptism is not magic, but it is the movement of God's love toward those who are suffering. In baptism God has joined the community of those who weep and mourn, tendering the hope of resurrection and life. I can offer no less than that.

Making Small Talk

A cousin of mine said to me a few months ago, "I couldn't do your job; you know, sitting around making small talk with people." Now this is a guy who has worked in hospitals for over 30 years and has surely been around chaplains. But he is clueless about what effective chaplains do. Yes, there is always a certain amount of "small talk," especially with patients who do not want to enter the valleys of personal disclosure, anxiety, fear, or loss.

Some people think a chaplain is like a professional mourner. Throughout history people have been paid to mourn the death of someone they are not related to. In Western cultures they were found standing outside the door of the deceased's house, funeral parlor, or church dressed in black. Sometimes they followed the funeral procession. Professional mourners are still found in the Middle East and parts of Asia. A chaplain is not a professional mourner. Effective chaplains journey with a patient and family through the dying process and bereavement. That requires quiet presence, education of families, emotional and spiritual direction. Sometimes that means encouraging decisions like durable powers of attorney, "Do Not Resuscitate," hospice care, and memorial arrangements.

Don't gloss over the word presence. Sometimes the chaplain is the only calm presence in a room of crash carts, bustling lab and EKG technicians, and panicked patients. The chaplain's presence, even without saying a word, pushes back the chaos and allows space for centeredness, space to take a deep breath, space to absorb all that is happening to changing lives.

Some people think of a chaplain as something akin to the "Candy Striper" model. Perhaps you remember the days when Candy Stripers delivered flowers and cards to rooms, pushed library carts from room to room, or candy carts with gum, chocolates, cigarettes, and newspapers. I have a very good sense of humor and hope that I bring joy to people. But an effective chaplain is not a Candy Striper offering faint optimism to our patients. The purpose I hope to bring to every patient is one of dignity, even in the most desperate circumstance. Maybe such hope is the presence of God. Maybe that hope is the still small voice that allows people to say, "Goodbye, I love you."

There are also those who think that a chaplain is just another visitor, stopping by someone's room on the way home from work, hoping to cheer them up. People sometimes visit family and friends in a hospital out of a sense of obligation. Local clergy, if they visit their parishioners at all, often do so because that is their job. Of course there are some pastors who visit out of a deep well of compassion. But the hospital chaplain is not just another visitor. The chaplain is part of the health care team. Nearly everyday I receive written referrals from hospitalists and other physicians regarding their patients. Referrals may also be verbal. Nurses, social workers, and therapists will also suggest I visit particular patients. I take all of these referrals very seriously and put them at the top of my list. I make a point of not leaving the hospital until I have called on those patients. Where appropriate I may do a spiritual assessment that becomes part of their medical records or chart notes on my conversation with and observations of a patient. These tools may sometimes make recommendations that range from psychiatric consultations to family interventions to referrals to the patient's minister if they give me permission to do that.

All of these are matters of the soul. Everything that I do is part of spiritual care. Patrick Fleming has written, "We all have the soul force within us to spring back to form when life tries to knock us down." Our patients never go home whole without tending to the soul force within them.

*****

My work as chaplain also includes serving on the Emergency Management Committee, the Diabetes Education Advisory Board, the Crisis Response Team, the Medical Ethics Committee, and I make a small contribution to New Employee Orientation. I co-facilitate the Palliative Care Team. I respond to all codes, from a "code black" to STEMI alerts in the Emergency Department. I serve on Wichita State University's Institutional Review Board. Pastoral care and counseling of hospital staff can take a great deal of time on any given day. I also officiate at their weddings, funerals, and baptisms. I send a birthday card to every employee with a handwritten note. I write a monthly newspaper column and speak at local churches on issues such as grief or suicide prevention.

I cannot tell you what a typical day is like. There are some days when I spend one half of my shift in the Intensive Care Unit or Emergency Department. There are some days when the census is low and I can write or study.

You should also know what I do not do. I do not evangelize. Proselytizing is not only inappropriate but also immoral. Not for a moment would I want a patient to think that health care services would be denied or minimized if they did not "convert" or subscribe to my faith. That would be an abuse of power. It only follows that I do not argue religion or politics. I do not criticize the faith or practices of other religions. In fact, I do everything in my power to respect and honor those of other religious traditions and those who do not proclaim faith.

I participate in a lot of training and continuing education. This includes recertification in CPR, active shooter training, ethics, palliative care, and grief counseling certification.

From here I would like to share with you a selection of the weekly meditations that I share with our beloved staff, which I call *The Chaplain's Chart.* Each meditation is a tiny glimpse of the heart of my chaplaincy. This is the soul of everything I work at and everyone I work for.

The Heart of My Chaplaincy

The Chaplain's Chart – for the Week of August 6, 2012

You have probably heard of SAD – seasonal affective disorder. It is a form of depression that usually occurs during the late fall through winter. It is thought to be related to the loss of sunlight, and "light therapy" is offered as one form of treatment. Symptoms include anxiety, sadness, hopelessness, irritability, restlessness, fatigue, and a general loss of interest in just about everything.

I have come up with a new disorder that I call CAD – climatic affective disorder. Like SAD, CAD is fraught with anxiety, a sense of loss, fatigue, and hopelessness. It is the result of too much sunlight, heat, and wind, common across the central plains. I have noticed CAD in many of the people I work with here at the hospital and in my church congregations in Hesston and Wichita. I feel it when I get into my car after work and the temperature is 111 degrees.

The drought has caused many of us to give up on our gardens, where we spent so much time rototilling, planting, weeding, and watering. While the wheat harvest was generally good, corn and soy are virtually destroyed. Stockmen are selling off cattle because they cannot afford hay and corn to feed their animals. I bought hay last year for my horses at $40.00 for a large round bale. This year the cheapest I could find was $80.00. Five years ago a 50# sack of horse feed sold for over $11.00 and now sells for over $16.00. Last year the cost of household groceries rose about 3% and is expected to rise another 3-4% this year. And just last week I read an article that mentioned the desertification of the American plains that began last year.

Is it any wonder that we are all feeling just a little blue with the creeping feeling that things are just not right in our world? What are we to do?

I have noticed that most of us here respond with lightning speed in an emergency. All of our skills become highly focused when a patient crashes or a severe trauma is carted into the emergency department. I love you for that and deeply respect you for such work.

The challenge for us, both in the hospital and in the larger community, is to reach deep down into our reserves to strengthen ourselves for the long haul. We must dive into the well of our deepest being to bring refreshment to people in our homes, our hospital, and our community. It is like what we have to do in the case of a catastrophic illness that might take months to travel its course.

We do not yet fully appreciate the challenges of climate change. We may only now begin to see the subtle shifts that will reshape our lives. We may not have the means to reverse it or even stop it. We can only live our lives and engage our relationships with grace. Thomas Merton wrote that we must, "Let go of all that seems to suggest getting somewhere, being someone, having a name and a voice, following a policy and directing people in "my" ways. What matters is to love."

I know you can do that. I have seen it in you on the hottest days of the year.

Much love to you all,
Chaplain Gary Blaine

The Chaplain's Chart – for the Week of August 13, 2012

"Georgia" lingered for days. I came to work each morning expecting a notice in my box that she had expired. She teased us with life for days at a time. When she was able she declared that she had no religious affiliation, but I found her to be one of the most centered people I have ever met, even as the pneumonia filled her lungs. Georgia was at peace with herself. Kindness and an abiding patience were her ever present companions. Family and friends packed her room and spilled out into the hallway. They spoke of the many children she had raised, some not her own. She was a true friend and guide to those who were lost and perplexed. Georgia was their anchor. One of her great grandsons wept openly as I hugged him.

One keeper of the vigil said to me, "I'm really angry with God right now. I don't know why he just doesn't take her, you know, end the suffering. It just isn't right."

Alfred North Whitehead once said that all theology eventually wrecks on the shoals of suffering. I have found that during times of grief and loss we ask questions that have no answers. We rail against the heavens and doubt the love of God. I have known many people who have said to me, "I lost all faith in God when my mother died," or "I used to believe in God until my spouse had an affair and left me."

Why are we so shocked and angered? I think part of the answer is the fact that we have not made peace with the fact that God is the Author of life and death. It's all in the package of being human. Job declared, "Naked I came from my mother's womb, and naked shall I return there; the Lord gave, and the Lord has taken away; blessed be the name of the Lord." (1:21) Death has always been a part of the design of life, long before the serpent ever had a conversation with Adam and Eve. Nowhere does it say in Genesis that Eden excluded death.

So where is the love of God in all of that? I believe that the love of God does not exempt us from pain and death. I also believe that God is the love that sees us through the giving and taking away, our coming and going, our inhale and exhale, the ebb and flow of our being. God's love is Georgia's family surrounding her with appreciation and deep respect, and refusing to let her die alone. God's love is the tender care that doctors, nurses, and other hospital staff gave to her. God's love is the gentle tear that rolled down the cheeks of the 10-year-old great grandson. God's love is her memory that will find a place in our hearts as we learn from her how to die with dignity. God's love is the grace that took her through more than 80 years and will carry her forward into eternity.

Robert Friend wrote:

> They tell me I am going to die.
> Why don't I seem to care?
> My cup is full. Let it spill.

I invite you to go through this week spilling buckets of love and grace to all you encounter, the quick and the dying. Trust me, housekeeping won't mind.

Yours in faith,
Chaplain Gary Blaine

28

What we know is finally not enough. Yet, in every department in this hospital we are constantly learning and retraining. There are new medical procedures, new protocols for hazardous waste, new recipes, and new tax laws. Just think of the changes that have been made in CPR. When I first learned it as a Boy Scout the victim was placed on his/her stomach, arms were folded in front of their head, the mouth was opened and turned to one side. On our knees in front of the victim's head we pressed on his or her back and pulled his/her arms forward toward us. We had not heard of the Heimlich maneuver.

This is even true for your chaplain. For example, when I first learned about grief work the term "closure" was very popular. The rough idea was that we would help people through the stages of grief and bring them to closure. You still hear that word used quite a bit. We have had to rethink that idea and have realized it is wrong. People will always carry their losses in their hearts. We do not come to closure with the death of a child or loved one. We can learn how to carry that loss with dignity. We can learn to open our hearts to new love and loyal relationships. Oh yeah, we have also learned that the "stages" of death and dying are not so clean or mechanical as we once thought.

We retrain, relearn, and retool for many reasons. Sometimes it is a requirement that has come down to us from the federal government, or the department chair, or the CEO. Most of the time, we do it because we want to be competent care providers. We want to give our patients and their families the best care we can possibly offer. We love our work and we love the people we tend to and could not imagine giving them medical care that is slipshod or second rate.

In other words, our knowledge is driven by a moral directive. We are compelled by a moral imperative to treat other human beings with every skill and resource at our disposal. And if we think about it, every thing we do, every action that we take, every procedure we initiate is a moral choice. Even our attitude toward patients, their families, and one another has moral consequences.

And guess what? That is how God created us. In my faith tradition we say that we are made in the image of God. And that means that God made us moral agents from the very beginning. That little seed of consciousness, the spark of goodness that wants to flame, is the essence of God blossoming and burning in our souls. We learn new skills and grow in our competencies because it is the right thing to do. This applies to every one of us from housekeepers to surgeons. And because God has planted this divine seed of moral agency in every one of us, every one of you is a sacred being.

May God's grace bless each of you.

Chaplain Gary Blaine

The Chaplain's Chart – for the Week of October 1, 2012

A few weeks ago a visitor demanded to know, "Isn't it your job to bring patients to Jesus Christ as Lord and personal savior?" I told him that it was not. "Why not?" he asked. I explained that my primary responsibility was to bring comfort to all persons – patients, families, and hospital staff. I hope that I reflect the grace and courage of God, regardless of circumstances, prognoses, and even death. Furthermore, I never assume what another person's relationship with the Sacred might be. I never assume what their faith stance is or should be. Such assumptions often lead to judgments I cannot make. In fact, I serve many faith traditions on a daily basis, and I don't just mean Christian ones.

In his book, *The Problem of Pain*, C. S. Lewis wrote, "When pain is to be borne, a little courage helps more than much knowledge, a little human sympathy more than courage, and the least tincture of the love of God more than all." May I be the least tincture of the love of God. Salvation ultimately evolves out of God's love and it is the responsibility of the local churches, mosques, and synagogues to bring such messages.

I had a vision the other day. I was standing in the center of a carousel. I was stationary but the carousel was circling around me. Instead of lions, horses, zebras, and tigers, were the faces of patients I had seen that day. Each was as different as the circus animals – a newborn, an old one, a dying one, a rehab patient taking her first

30

steps in weeks, a worried face in the surgical waiting room, a child asleep in his mother's arms in the emergency department, and the smile of a nurse who seemed genuinely happy to see me on the floor. It occurred to me in this flight of imagination that these were the many faces of God. It is the mystery that we encounter at Susan B. Allen every day.

Even death unfolds as the mystery of God. Perhaps Emily Dickinson said it best:

> Pass now to the Rendezvous of Light
> Pangless except for us
> Who must slowly ford the Mystery
> Which thou hast leaped across

It is my job to behold the mystery of human suffering, the profound compassion and care that everyone in this hospital hopes to bring to our patients, and the ultimate hope that lays beyond it all. I am sure that somewhere in this hospital there is tincture of iodine. May we all be a tincture of love and grace to all whom we serve.

And don't forget that I am here to serve you too!

Your Chaplain, *Gary*

The Chaplain's Chart – for the Week of November 5, 2012

I was taking a Clinical Pastoral Education course in seminary back in the 1970's at Emory University Hospital. I visited a patient who was 86 years-old. She was from Wales and had a beautiful brogue. Sadly, she was blind and suffered from heart disease, cancer, and shingles. Having requested Holy Communion, I set up bread and chalice on her hospital bed tray. I read through the liturgy, beginning with the prayer of Great Thanksgiving. My patient seemed to sleep through that part of it, but I was wrong. Right on cue she recited the Lord's Prayer. After blessing the bread and wine I served her. A beautiful smile spread across her face, and as if looking directly into my soul she said, "Oh, reverend that was wonderful. Isn't God good?" Say that line over again trilling the letter "r" in a rich Welsh fashion.

On another occasion, this was Christmas Eve, I was serving communion in the Hall County (GA) jail. Most of the inmates elected to participate because it gave them a chance to get out of their cell. One young man sat with the other inmates around the large table, a snide smirk on his face. He had been arrested for grand larceny. In the Eucharistic prayer I led them singing, "Holy, holy, holy Lord, God of power and might…" The prisoners sang back each line with me. Before consecrating the bread and wine we sang, "Silent Night, Holy Night." As we sang, "round yon Virgin, Mother and Child," I looked up to see tears running down the face of that young man.

Referring to the breaking of bread at the Last Supper, Jesus said, "Do this in remembrance of me." The use of the word "remember" in the Greek New Testament does not only mean an act of recall. It also means to "make present." And in the Christian tradition, the breaking of bread and drinking of wine is about entering the presence of what is holy. By breaking bread and sharing the cup, Christians enter the drama of loving others beyond all reckoning. Ed Ostrom wrote a prayer, "Communion." that captures the power of the Eucharist:

> As I eat the bread and drink the wine,
> May Your sweet presence occupy my mind.
> Come O Lord commune with me this hour,
> Impart to me Your strength and power,
> My life must be your broken bread each day.[2]

You sense in Ed's poem the immediacy and intimacy of Holy Communion. And that is why I think it is a sacrament so often appropriate for hospital patients and staff. The Eucharist was not going to give that beautiful Welsh woman eyesight or a new heart. It was not going to break that young prisoner out of jail. Indeed, he was convicted and sent to the state penitentiary. But in the moment of communion we enter into the sacred space of unconditional love, forgiveness, restoration, and wholeness. Our personhood is given

---

[2] Ed Orstrom, "Communion," *Helium* at: http://www.helium.com/items/2032086-poetry-communion.

a new promise of what it means to be made in the image of God. It reminds us of all that is good and possible as children on this earth. If you are blind and dying of cancer, that can be a precious moment.

At the very least I hope you know that I make Holy Communion available to any patient who asks for it. I am not sure what the practice has been in the past, but would like to hear suggestions from you. Is it a pastoral care practice that might have greater use for patients and staff? Let me know. In the meantime remember – there's that word again – I am here for you.

Your Chaplain,
Gary

The Chaplain's Chart – for the Week of November 19, 2012

Thanksgiving is my very favorite celebration. For a minister it is the least contentious and the least pretentious holiday. I appreciate the simple opportunity to give thanks and to celebrate food, family, and freedom. German theologian and mystic, Meister Eckhart (1260-1328) said, "If the only prayer you ever say in your entire life is thank you, it will be enough."

When I was a child my family went to my grandparents' house for Thanksgiving. My grandmother asked every member of the family what special dish they would like for her to prepare. My uncle Leon wanted rice with gravy, my dad requested biscuits, and my aunt hoped for sweet potato soufflé. The list was a lot longer and my grandmother prepared them all, along with the turkey, oyster dressing, and pies. When my great grandfather was still alive he gave the table blessing. We never really understood what he was mumbling and did not know when he was finished until he said, "Pass the biscuits."

We did not have iPhones, iPods, iPads, or MP3 devices. I may have had a transistor radio but I had enough sense to leave it at home. My grandparents had a television but it was not turned on. Instead, stories were told about growing up in the Depression and World War II. That was where I learned about my family's history and the values that shape my character. There was talk about American history, the Civil War and its impact on Southerners, and politics. Franklin D. Roosevelt and Harry Truman were favorites but we were fascinated by the young Jack Kennedy. Martin Luther King Jr. and the Civil Rights movement became part of the conversation in the early 1960's. We did not know what to make of him. On the one hand he represented a disturbing challenge to the prejudices of the Deep South, but we could not dismiss the power of his preaching.

We all went home with plates of leftovers, though I do not recall that there was ever a single extra biscuit.

I hope that over this holiday you and your family and friends will have the opportunity to gather, give thanks, share delicious food, and tell stories. Yes, that means the kids (and adults for that matter) will have to turn off their electronic devices and hear one another. My sister-in-law likes to have everyone bring a favorite poem to share at the table. I hope that you will all be blessed and may God protect you from that plague I keep hearing about, "Black Friday." It sounds frightening. I close with these words from the hymn, "Now Thank We All Our God," by Johann Cruger:

Now thank we all our God, with heart and hands and voices,
Who wondrous things hath done, in whom His world rejoices;
Who from our mothers' arms Hath bless'd us on our way,
With countless gifts of love, and still is ours today.

O may this bounteous God through all our life be near us,
With ever joyful hearts, and blessed peace to cheer us;
And keep us in His grace, and guide us when perplexed;
And free us from all ills, in this world and the next.

Your Chaplain,
Gary

The Chaplain's Chart – for the Week of November 26, 2012

We had a wonderful trip to Columbus, visiting Mimi's mother who is 88. She resides in an assisted living community and is doing quite well. Gloria has just given up her Eucharistic Ministry of taking communion to Roman Catholic shut-ins in her parish. But every day she visits all of her neighbors making sure that everyone is up and running. I am reminded of a comment I heard recently, "Every day I wake up on this side of the grass is a good day." Gloria wants to make sure her neighbors are still on this side of the grass.

This Sunday is the first Sunday in Advent, the season of anticipation and expectation in the Christian tradition. I will begin a series of sermons, "Every Family is a Holy Family." Over the Thanksgiving weekend I was fortunate to witness sacred family moments. Lisa Van Dusen recently sent me one such memory. She wrote a beautiful story about her mother who has Alzheimer's disease. Visiting her mother in the hospital, Lisa wrote about the sadness of having a mother who does not recognize her own daughter. But as her mother talked Lisa made a decision. "I decided to try to connect with her in a way I never have before. Instead of trying to pull her back into lucidity I entered her world, her reality, and spent the most wonderful time with my mother. Instead of patiently half-listening to her repeated stories, I probed her memories and we took a trip back in time. It was a wonderful trip."

They talked of growing up in a country house in Nebraska, speculated about the place of family in heaven and what purpose they might serve there. At the close of their conversation Lisa's mom turned and smiled at her. "This has been wonderful. This has made a difference…This has been a wonderful adventure. It is wonderful to talk to someone who you have known for a long time. How long have I known you? You are my very best friend and I love you."

Lisa wrote, "I sat quietly as the nurse cared for my mother, surprised at my own reaction. I would have expected to be upset that Mom did not recognize me, but really, it didn't bother me. I realized that as time has gone on I have grown confortable being with my mother as whomever she is at any given moment."

Thank you, Lisa, for sharing your beautiful story with me. You remind me what pastoral care is all about – entering into the stories of other people and being claimed by sacred memory and the values and purposes that make us wholly human. Whether I am recognized or not is finally not as important as their wonder filled adventures, camaraderie, and shared love.

One of my favorite family moments from this past weekend is that of two little girls, I would guess six and four, who came down to the breakfast bar at the motel. The little one asked her grandmother, "Can I have a donut?" Grandmother answered, "Yes." The little girl squealed, "Oh! This is a great day!" I hope that you have a great day.

Your Chaplain,

Gary

The Chaplain's Chart – for the Week of January 1, 2013

I believe that too often the Christian tradition has focused on what is wrong with people. I certainly agree that there are many flaws in the human character. However, that is not our first identity. Some people argue that we are defined by "original sin," and thus are corrupted from our birth. I believe that God first defined us in God's own image. Despite the story of the serpent, the rebellion of Adam and Eve, and their alienation from the garden; nowhere is it written that the image of God is removed from our essential being. To be made in God's image means that we are first creatures of light and love and moral discernment. I believe that this is our true nature. Thus, I believe in original goodness.

Yes, we seem to have worked very hard at hiding the light under the basket of greed, smothered love in the smoke of fear, and nearly choked the life out of our responsibility to one another. But that does not mean that the life, love, and righteousness that God gave us in the beginning is completely lost. We certainly need restoration and reconciliation, but I do not doubt it was there in the first place and do not believe that it can be completely eradicated.

Why is this important to our work in the hospital or my work as a chaplain? Healing is about the wholeness of a person's being – body, mind, and soul. There is a clear relationship between our ability to heal and the well-being of a person's soul. This is especially true when we think about the role of death in the healing process. I am always asking patients what inner strengths they bring to their disease, suffering, and death. What brings them solace? Where is the anchor of their being? My biggest concern is the patient who cannot identify a single source of strength that will see them through recovery and even through their dying.

An example is an 88-year-old who had been referred to hospice care. She was angry with the hospital because we are not going to offer her any other treatments. She agreed that all treatments had failed to bring her back to health and somehow imagined that we had yet one more treatment that would heal her. When I asked her what resources she had to live out her dying days there was a long pause. "I can't think of any," she said sadly. I then asked if there was anything that would bring her comfort. Again she paused, looked down, and said, "No."

I cannot presume there is a "correct" answer to my question. It is not my place to judge the spiritual reserves that a person can draw from to see them through the end of their lives. My job is to help them draw on those strengths or rediscover them, whatever they may be. This is something that you have to do as well. I watch you deal with difficult patients, distraught families, staff tensions, and the yuck factor in any hospital setting. You know what I am talking about – incontinence, vomit, waste, blood, *et.al.*

I know that deep down inside of every person who works here there is an eternal worth that shines, loves, and treats people in just and righteous ways. You probably don't think about it most of the time, but I see it in you every day.

William Blake wrote:

> Joy and woe are woven fine,
> A clothing for the soul divine:
> Under every grief and pine
> Runs a joy with silken twine.

So it is I seek the silken twine that threads its way in every grief and sorrow. I hope that yours is a blessed New Year. And don't forget that I am here for you.

Your Chaplain,
Gary

Struggle, and even suffering, comes to every human being. It is an unavoidable reality of our lives. The question is what will that suffering make of us? What can we learn from it? I have known people who are angry and bitter with the trials and tribulations that come their way. Some feel that their lives are cursed because of the slightest inconvenience. I have also known people who have endured great hardship and emerge as women and men of poise and compassion.

The very first funeral that I officiated was that of a five-day-old infant. Thomas Lee was born in perfect health at an Army Hospital in Texas. He contracted a staph infection and died. Thomas Lee was named after his mother's brother who was killed in an automobile accident at the age of sixteen. His mother's youngest brother was born with a severe cleft pallet. Yet this family was as warm and loving as any I have ever known. They always made me feel very welcome. The coffee pot was always on and there was a place for me at their gracious table board, any time, any day. Thirty-eight years later I pray that I may be as compassionate and hospitable as the Haynes family.

I am reminded of the poem by R. B. Hamilton:

> I walked a mile with Pleasure;
> She chattered all the way,
> But left me none the wiser
> For all she had to say.
> I walked a mile with Sorrow
> And ne'er a word said she;
> But oh, the things I learned from her
> When Sorrow walked with me.

Life is always teaching me things, why shouldn't struggle and sorrow? It reminds me of the often told story of the little boy who found the chrysalis of a Monarch butterfly. He took the branch it was attached to and put it in an aquarium. Several weeks later he noticed the chrysalis moving. He took it out of the aquarium and onto his desk. For hours he watched as the cocoon slowly cracked open. The emerging butterfly was working hard to break out of its shell.

After a couple of hours the boy decided he would help the butterfly. He went to his sister's room and took her dissecting kit for high school biology. Fitting the sharp pointed scissors very carefully into the chrysalis he carefully cut away the cast. The beautiful butterfly stood grandly on the boy's desk waving its wings.

The boy opened the window fully expecting the butterfly to wing its way to freedom. Indeed, it looked as though it would fly away any moment. But it did not. It stood on the desk unable to take flight. Though well intentioned, the boy did not understand that the struggle of the butterfly was essential to strengthening its wings. It would never be able to fly because it was not strong enough.

Whenever we struggle through the flight of our lives we have to choose how suffering and sorrow will discipline us. We can choose guilt and anger or we can choose growth and the discipline of character. We can choose to be bitter or wonder how God can help forge our suffering into strength.

We are here, together, to struggle and grow strong.
Gary

The Chaplain's Chart – for the Week of March 11, 2013

I don't know about you, but boy am I glad last week is over! It was our first "normal" week after two weeks of snow and disrupted schedules. Some of us came in last Monday tired from working too hard, worried about lost time at work, or sore from shoveling out driveways packed with snow – twice! And while our census was not high, we served a lot of patients who were very sick with prognoses that were dire. Let's be honest, there was crabbiness in the air with a bit of grumbling, well tossed with frustration.

There are noncompliant patients who are back in the hospital for the umpteenth time who have not exercised, managed their diets, quit smoking, continued with physical therapy, taken their medication, or kept their doctors' appointments. We know very well that there are intervention strategies that will return them to health or strengthen their quality of life, but they do not comply. We anxiously watch their health decline to the point where we can no longer effect recovery. We also witness patients with congestive heart failure, COPD, or cancer move to ever higher levels of disease where there is no turning back. And then there are family dynamics that actively sabotage a patient's health by sneaking "Chips Ahoy" into the diabetic patient's room, or bring into the hospital narcotics that the patient was taking at home. And who doesn't love working with a family in rabid denial about the health and longevity of the patient and demanding treatment services that will do nothing to change the outcome? Mention "comfort care," or "palliative care," or "hospice" and they are demanding a new doctor, and "keep that troublesome chaplain out of our room."

When we are confronted with noncompliance we are, at the very least, frustrated. We know of several different health options that could restore the patient but the patient refuses to cooperate. That makes us angry. I'm not saying it never happens, but I have not witnessed any one of us blowing up with a patient or the patient's family. I think, rather, that we tend to take it out on each other. We huff, roll our eyes, stomp off muttering, or talk about each other in the break room or cafeteria. Or we take it out on ourselves, eating an extra cookie(s) at lunch, skipping exercise because we're tired, or translating our anger into headaches or heartburn. Don't worry; it happens in every place of business, office, agency, and institution that I know of. Anger is a normal human emotion that often erupts when we sense that things are out of control and everything we have tried to regain control fails. There is nothing like the noncompliant patient to push our anger buttons.

The hard truth is that every patient in his or her right mind is an autonomous person who has the right to decline our best medical advice and practice. To put it another way, they have the right to choose noncompliance. No amount of anger on our part can abridge the autonomy of the patient.

The last thing I would try to tell you is, "Don't get angry." Anger cannot be helped. What we can do with anger is put it into perspective. Hold anger up to the light of our highest professional standards and know that we have done all in our power to serve our patients with compassion. Hold anger up to the light of autonomy and honor the freedom of human beings to make choices about their health. You have privileged a patient and their family by respecting their autonomy. Then move on to the next patient you serve. Take a walk or have a cup of coffee with a confidant. Lift up that person to God and remember that each of us is finally in those everlasting hands. If you have to eat the extra cookie, OK. Just recalibrate your treadmill to take off those extra calories. Deal with your anger before it deals with you. Heed the words of St. Paul, "Do not let the sun go down while you are still angry." (Ephesians 4:26)

Remember that I am here for you.

Your Chaplain,

Gary Blaine

The Chaplain's Chart – for the Week of March 18, 2013

Last week was quite a week for our Roman Catholic friends. Pope Francis I was elected to the papacy and on Sunday, St. Patrick's Day, was honored all across the church universal. Between white smoke and green shamrocks it was quite a week of celebration and hope. From Monday through Sunday I heard many Catholics, young and old, say something like, "Now we have a reason to go back to church."

The new pope deliberately chose the name Francis in homage to the saint of Assisi. St. Francis of Assisi is well known for his kindness to animals and his choice of "holy poverty" with the implication that the church ought to be a poor church, using its resources primarily to benefit the poor. The new pope is said to be a man of deep humility who often took funds that would give added comfort to his lifestyle as a cardinal and shared those funds with the poor. Thus he did not live in the lavish estate of the cardinal in Argentina but in a simple apartment. He cooked his own meals. Rather than use the limousine available to him he rode the bus back and forth to work. After his election he commented that he wanted a poor church for poor people.

That is a wonderful sentiment, is it not? I wonder how far his leadership will take the church in that direction. There will be many who will resist him. It is a fact that all institutions tend to amass property, liquid assets, and power over the centuries. And it is a fact that they are reluctant to give those up. I have served many churches in my ministry who were more concerned about the new carpet in the parlor than the impoverished who lived in the shadow of the church's steeple. I never served a church that had a fight about how to best serve low income families. Rather, they fought about the budget, the hiring and firing of staff, and the new building addition.

Though written in the 20th century, I find the "Prayer of St. Francis" consistent with everything we know about him and from his writings. It is certainly consistent with a life of humility and service. I pray it at least once a day:

> Lord, make me an instrument of thy peace,
> Where there is hatred, let me sow love;
> Where there is injury, pardon;
> Where there is doubt, faith;
> Where they is despair, hope;
> Where there is darkness, light;
> Where there is sadness, joy.
> O Divine Master, grant that
> I may not so much seek
> To be consoled, as to console;
> Not so much to be understood, as
> To understand; not so much to be
> Loved as to love;
> For it is in giving that we receive;
> It is in pardoning that we are pardoned;
> It is in dying that we awaken to eternal life.

No matter the task that each of us performs here at the hospital, we can all be instruments of peace and love; regardless of the prognosis of a patient, the burden of their pain, or the suffering of their families.

Your Chaplain,
Gary Blaine

This is Holy Week for Christians throughout the world. It began yesterday with Palm Sunday, remembering Jesus' entry into Jerusalem astride a donkey. The donkey in the ancient world symbolizes an animal of peace, whereas the horse is thought to be an animal of war. The people lined the streets waving palm branches and shouting "Hosanna, blessed is he who comes in the name of the Lord." The palm branch was seen as a symbol for royalty, and the triumph and victory of the Roman Empire. For a common Jew like Jesus to ride a donkey into Jerusalem claiming a royal peace beyond the grasp of Caesar was nothing less than a challenge to the power of Rome. And the very people who shouted "Hosanna" would be shouting "Crucify him!" in less than a week.

At first glance the long arm of Caesar seems to have crushed the man and message of the Carpenter. By Friday Jesus gasped his last breath on the cross. Asphyxiation is the real cause of death for those who are crucified. The weight of the body on the upper chest makes the condemned suffocate. Breaking the legs makes the weight and pressure on the lungs ever worse. This method of execution was especially heinous to Jews who understood that the human breath is the very breath of life that God breathed into Adam. Because of the importance of this meaning Jews will not eat the meat of an animal that has been strangled to death. Where is the triumph of Jesus' disciples now? In fact, they all ran away and hid.

But Caesar's royal power does not win out. On Easter Sunday morning the tomb is empty, despite the posting of Roman Centurions at the grave. How would you like to be the guard who had to fill out the paperwork on that "critical incident?" The celebration of the resurrection is the triumph of God's grace over imperialism, God's love over every form of oppression, including death.

As I wrote earlier, every day at Susan B. Allen is a holy one. While none of us here is a messiah, we all watch hope enter our doors in the expectation of healing and a fresh start on life. Sometimes we witness those hopes crushed. People die here. Lifestyles are often unalterably changed to something less than the

43

patient imagined. We also witness new sight for the blind, a mended arm or leg, and the fact that some get off their beds and walk out of here. Death and resurrection is our daily bread. We cannot be like the disciples who will run away and hide from the stillborn baby, the stage four cancer, the massive heart attack, or the loss of sanity. Like the faithful women at the cross we tend all who suffer, work for their restoration, and trust that nothing can separate any of them from the love of God. We celebrate these little resurrections understanding that the day after Easter is just another Monday. Holy Week begins anew.

I hope that this Holy Week is a blessing for you all, and never forget that I am here for you.

Your Chaplain,
Gary

The Chaplain's Chart – for the Week of April 15, 2013

C. S. Lewis wrote *Chiefly on Prayer* where he challenges us to recover our "off stage life." The fact is, that we are often on the stage of life, playing a role scripted by someone else, costumed and made up with various powders, eyeliners, and lipstick. Every once in a while I will catch an old western movie where the hero's face is powdered, eye brows and lashes artificially darkened, with rouged cheeks and rose shaded lips. Their makeup is so over the top they look like Japanese kabuki actors.

Actors are playing to an audience as they take their cues from each other, or a drama coach in the wing. Actors play to each other and sometimes to members in the orchestra pit. All of us have a role to play at Susan B. Allen. If we were giving credits at the end of a shift it might scroll down with the role and the actor: Hospitalist played by Dr. Ruben Garcia, Director of the Emergency Department played by Robin Dean, Nurse played by Kristin Jones, and so on. Sometimes the names are lost and we are only the title roles. I was the minister of a rural congregation. People did not call me "Gary" or "Rev. Blaine." My name was "Preacher" on every occasion. But these are not the only roles that we are given in life. We are parents, significant others, fishing buddies, pee-wee baseball coaches, grandmas/pas, and *Et al.* With all of these roles there are expectations, job descriptions, and critics.

These are identity consuming roles and sometimes we make the mistake of thinking that our role is the most important thing about us. We judge ourselves and others on how well we perform. And when the reviews come in and the critics rage we scurry to blame others – the writers, set designers, other actors, and the critics themselves. ("They never understood my art.")

Lewis argues that we cannot escape the roles we play. Our mistake is to give them ultimate importance. When it comes to our relationship with God we have to let go of the scripts we have been handed, take off the grease paint and costumes, dim the stage lights, and send the orchestra home. No Academy Award gives us standing with God. Authentic faith presents our real selves to the Creator naked and vulnerable and yet full of possibilities.

But that is not all. Authentic prayer comes when we let go of all of the "roles" and images that we have given to God. You see, the temptation is for us to pray to or worship our idea of God. We know that the Holy Spirit is working in our lives when all of our assumptions, doctrines, images, and theologies about God are shattered. We stand before the raw power of Creativity and its fire consumes all of the pine boxes of our religious presumption. One of the most prominent theologians in Christian history was Thomas Aquinas. When asked about the importance of his work, he replied, "It reminds me of straw."

It sounds crazy and most of us are not willing to try it but I dare say that what makes a good church a great church or a good hospital a great hospital is when we allow our vulnerability to enter the stages of our lives. As scientific as we try to be, healing is still an art form. Medical protocols and regulations (and they are legion) do not absolutely conclude in good health. With every medical procedure there is risk, fear, hope, and factors beyond our control. About the time we think we are cool, calm, and professional a streak of panic bolts through our minds, our hands shake, and our eyes shed a tear. I worry about people who always have to be right, perfect, stay within the letter of the law, and never color outside the lines. With vulnerability comes the freedom of imagination and creativity.

You are wonderful people. I watch you work hard everyday. I am amazed at the level of your skill. I see the compassion you give to patients. I love you for that. I also see you get crabby, freeze up, wipe away a tear, and throw up your hands in exasperation. I love you for that too and wouldn't have you any other way. When we are vulnerable it means that there is a soft spot in our hearts, a portal for grace and forgiveness.

Your Chaplain, *Gary*

The Chaplain's Chart – for the Week of April 22, 2013

The events of this past week at the Boston Marathon and the explosion of the fertilizer plant in West Texas, brought to my mind Fr. Mychal Judge, chaplain for the New York Fire Department. On almost every photograph you see of Chaplain Judge he wears a beautiful and generous smile. Throughout his career he brought a great deal of comfort to firefighters and their families, through all of the human events known to every one of us. He was there for their weddings, baptisms, divorces, illnesses, and death. Fr. Judge was often seen on the streets of New York City offering the same love and care for street people, including the homeless, hungry, substance abusers, "working girls," and people with AIDS.

Two stories are often told about him. One is that he gave his winter coat to a homeless woman who was shivering with cold. "She needed it more than I did," he quipped. Another is his ministry with a man who was dying with AIDS. Fr. Judge was administering "last rites" to the man, anointing him with holy oils. The dying man asked, "Do you think that God hates me?" Fr. Judge brought the man into his arms, kissed him, and rocked him back and forth.

Some people think that Fr. Judge should be beatified, especially firefighters. Others do not hold that same opinion because Fr. Judge was a recovering alcoholic and there were rumors that he was a gay man.

When the Twin Towers were struck on 9/11/2001 Chaplain Judge went immediately to the site. Many other clergy also went there, but the Chaplain was the only one who entered the buildings. If you have seen the documentary *911,* there is footage of him standing in the lobby of the second tower. The Chaplain offered last rites to the dying and comforted those who had been injured in the attacks, first responders and people trying to escape. A large piece of cement hit Chaplain Judge on the head and he was killed. Several firefighters and citizens carried his body to St. Peter's Church and placed him at the altar. He is the first identified fatality of the 9/11 attacks.

On September 10, 2001 Chaplain Judge gave his last homily. In that homily is his prayer that I want to share with you in part:

"Thank you Lord for life. Thank you for love. Thank you for goodness. Thank you for work. Thank you for family. Thank you for friends. Thank you for every gift because we know that every gift comes from you, and without you, we have and are nothing."

The lore around the firehouse is that God took Chaplain Mychal Judge first so that he might lead all the others into God's eternal arms.

Don't forget that I am here for you, and that I am,
Your Chaplain, *Gary*

The Chaplain's Chart – for the Week of April 29, 2013

Around the third century there lived in the desert of Egypt a scattering of Christian hermits, monks, and ascetics. They are known as the "desert Fathers and Mothers." Amma Syncletica of Alexandria and Abba Anthony (The Great) are two of the most well known of the mothers and fathers. Their bits of wisdom are gathered in books, *Sayings of the Desert Fathers (and Mothers)*, which are still in print. Here is one such offering:

"A brother said to an old man: 'There were two brothers. One of them stays in his cell quietly, fasting for six days at a time, and imposing on himself a good deal of discipline and the other serves the sick. Which one of them is more acceptable to God?' The old man replied: 'Even if the brother who fasts six days were to hang himself by the nose, he could not equal the one who serves the sick.'"

I guess the desert heat and the isolation of these hermits cuts away all of the superfluities and makes one come right to the point. People can wrap themselves up in all kinds of piety but the fundamental question of faith is "whom do you serve?" In the Arthurian literature the question is put this way: "Who do you serve when you serve the Fisher King?" Jesus constantly calls upon his disciples to serve, feed, heal, and redeem the most vulnerable people in the community. Indeed, he quoted the prophet Isaiah in his first sermon announcing the purpose of his ministry: "The Spirit of the Lord is upon me because he has anointed me to bring good news to the poor. He has sent me to proclaim release to the captives and recovery of sight to the blind, to let the oppressed go free, and to proclaim the year of the Lord's favor."

A fundamental precept of Buddhism is to free the world from suffering. The First Mindfulness Training of Buddhist teacher Thich Nhat Hanh reads: "Aware of the suffering caused by the destruction of life, I am committed to cultivating compassion and learning ways to protect the lives of people, animals, plants, and minerals."

I bet that most people at Susan B. Allen, regardless of the work they do here, seldom think about the sacred nature of the work they do. Our mission statement reads, "The mission of Susan B. Allen Memorial Hospital is to provide compassionate, professional healthcare to the people we serve." This is an ancient and sacred mission. It reminds me of the parable of the "Great Banquet" in Luke's gospel (14:15-24). The master orders his servant to, "Go out at once into the streets and lanes of the town and bring in the poor, the crippled, the blind, and the lame." In the midst of the myriad of protocols, standards, regulations, and quality controls, we need to be reminded that our work here has ultimate value. Holy Stuff!

As your chaplain I am here, in part, to bear witness to "angels unawares," to "missionaries of wholeness," to the sacred current that flows out of your hands to the relief of suffering and pain. You may not be conscious of it but I see it often. None of us here are perfect, but I am truly thankful for the privilege of working in such a holy assembly.

I am your chaplain,
Gary

Did you ever wonder how buffalo ever managed to survive howling snowstorms or blizzards? Why is it more likely that they will survive as opposed to a herd of cattle? The difference is this. Cattle will keep their backsides into the wind and consequently will walk with the storm, keeping them exposed for longer periods of time. Buffalo will face the storm, walk into it, and consequently be in the storm for less time.

None of us like blizzards. Like cattle we are inclined to turn away from them and run, not understanding that we will only keep ourselves in the wind and frigid wet that much longer. The same thing is true with our relationships. We find ourselves facing a conflict, or even a storm, and we want to run away. Like the cattle we find that such behavior only makes matters worse and we struggle longer and harder than we need to.

Most of us avoid conflict. We don't want to have difficult conversations because we are afraid that people will not like us, we might get in trouble with our supervisor, or things will only get worse. In fact when we avoid the difficult conversations things will get worse. Misunderstanding, frustration, and anger build up. Our anxiety distorts our perceptions and we find ourselves questioning not only the other person's behaviors but their motives as well. We are also tempted to talk to other people about the issues and gossips play on every worry.

The first rule in conflict management is to deal with the conflict at the lowest possible level. The longer we postpone those difficult conversations the deeper the conflict grows, sometimes to the point of irreparable damage. It is false humility that imagines that we are being patient, forgiving, or long-suffering when we are conflicted with someone and refuse to engage them in conversations about the issues that separate us.

Part of my work as chaplain is to engage the difficult conversations. Generally this means speaking with a patient and/or his/her family about catastrophic illness, dying and death. We can use all kinds of euphemistic language like "end of life care," or "palliative care," or even "hospice care" if we are talking about the ways and means of bringing life to its end with the greatest comfort and management of symptoms. But we cannot avoid the reality that this life is ending. I am reminded of the person who had stage 4 COPD. When I asked him about that diagnosis he replied, "I don't think there are any stages in COPD."

"Well, actually there are," I began. We talked a long time. In such times as these I might expect tears. Some family members may get upset with me and not be happy that I was being so "negative." "You should only think happy thoughts," someone once exclaimed. And just to drive this point home, research continues to inform us that dying children need to talk about it.

May I suggest that we really care for one another – we really respect each other – when we have the difficult conversations. Notice I did not say text or email each other. You can only do that if you are writing something like, "I would love to have a chance to talk with you. What would be a good time for you?" Difficult conversations mean that you have to take time, focus on the issues, make eye contact, listen deeply, and keep options open for future conversations. Building trust is what a difficult conversation is all about. It is not about winning, proving a point, or diminishing the other in any possible way.

Before my son was deployed to Afghanistan we had lunch in a sushi bar in Detroit. We talked about what he would want me to do in the event he was wounded or killed. The conversation was intense and quite detailed. Fortunately I never had to deal with either event. A psychologist I know thought that was a horrible conversation. She was wrong and I told her so. It was one of the most honest and loving conversations Chris and I have ever had.

I am your Chaplain,
Gary

The Chaplain's Chart – for the Week of May 20, 2013

Leslie R. Smith tells the story of the famous preacher, Charles H. Spurgeon, who was out calling on his country parishioners. He came to one farm and saw a large weather vane. On it was painted these words, "God is Love." Spurgeon asked the farmer, "Do you mean God's love changes every time the wind blows?"

"No," replied the farmer, "I mean God loves us no matter which way the wind blows."

There is no telling which way the wind is blowing at Susan B. Allen, especially in areas like the Emergency Department and Intensive Care Unit. And it is true for every other department: A child is born and one is miscarried; a wound is healed and a wounded one dies; someone is admitted and someone is discharged, often at the same time. There are all kinds of hopes and disappointments between life and death. Sometimes there are gentle breezes that lift the window curtains and bring the scent of freshly mowed grass. Sometimes there are straight line winds that blow down an outbuilding or lift the roof off a house.

Sadly, there are some people who think that God makes the gentle winds blow for good people and the windstorms blow as punishment for others. I believe the winds blow for good or ill and on the just and the wicked. The issue is not why the winds blow. The question is who sustains us no matter which way the wind blows or by what force.

I believe that God is with us on a breezy summer afternoon and in the gales of tornado or blizzard. In the words of John Greenleaf Whittier:

> I know not what the future hath
> Of marvel or surprise,
> Assured alone that life and death
> His mercy underlies.
>
> I know not where His islands lift
> Their fronded palms in air;
> I only know I cannot drift
> Beyond His love and care.

My work as your chaplain is to watch the weathervane, not to see which way the wind is blowing, but to discern the love of God in the sweet breath of life as well as the tempest of trauma and catastrophic disease. My work as your chaplain is to watch the wheat rustle and the trees bow in your hands as you comfort and heal. Oh, yes, I see God fluttering and blowing there every day.

Remember, I am here for you.

Your Chaplain,

Gary

The Chaplain's Chart – for the Week of June 3, 2013

My theology can easily be summed up: "The love of God is greater than our sin, past and present," and, "God is with us." The love of God predicates all that God does in human history. The incarnation of God's love is God's will for all of creation, including every one of us. And it is important to understand that the incarnation of God's love is present with us, right here, right now.

Having said all of that, the challenge for me is to find the presence of God in every nook and cranny of our material existence. In his book, *God Hides in Plain Sight*, Dean Nelson suggests that the presence of the Creator, Redeemer, and Sustainer is right before our eyes. God's fingerprints and footprints are everywhere. Our spiritual journey is the quest to see Who is in front of us. That is not only my spiritual work but my chaplaincy work as well.

So if you see me with a flashlight and magnifying glass in the Emergency Department, or up on TLC (geropsych unit), or in the kitchen I am looking for the evidence of God. About the time I think I have God cornered in Housekeeping I get a call to the ICU where doctors are trying to intubate a patient whose blood oxygen percent is in the 50's. And then the other day I shared the anguish of another doctor over a child's cancer prognosis.

Always the question is, "Where is the compassion?" I ask, "Where is the love of God?" in any relationship, conversation, or action in this hospital. Everything unfolds in the presence of Grace, even when we are not so graceful, or as skilled as we hope to be. And along with that my work is to center myself in the Sacred Presence in the cafeteria, with the family of a dying one, and in the needs of patients and staff. I think of "Lines Written in Kensington

Gardens," by the English poet Matthew Arnold. You may know this poem as "Calm Soul of All Things," which can be sung to Tallis' canon:

> Calm soul of all things! Make it mine
> To feel, amid the city's jar,
> That there abides a peace of thine,
> Man did not make, and cannot mar!
>
> The will to neither strive nor cry,
> The power to feel with others give!
> Calm, calm me more! Nor let me die
> Before I have begun to live.

I hope I am that for you – before all theology or psychology, before all doctrine or creed, and before all scripture and ritual.

I am your chaplain,
Gary

The Chaplain's Chart – for the Week of June 17, 2013

One of my favorite evening prayers was written by St. Augustine. I often say it before going to sleep.

> "Watch thou, dear Lord, with those who wake, or watch, or weep tonight, and give Thine angels charge over those who sleep. Tend Thy sick, O Lord Christ. Rest Thy weary ones. Bless Thy dying ones. Soothe Thy suffering ones. Pity Thine afflicted ones. Shield Thy joyous ones. And all, for Thy love's sake. Amen."

It reminds me of all of the living and dying that takes place at a time we often think of as restful sleep. There are many who do not sleep, but lie in bed worrying about loved ones or thinking of the tests and challenges of the morrow. There are those who are watching the rise and fall of a sick one's breath or waiting for a teenager to come home well past curfew. There are those who will weep with the passing of a loved one or the unwelcome news of family tragedy.

The prayer also reminds me of you, who tend the sick ones, the weary ones, the dying ones, and the suffering ones. I wonder if you might consider the possibility that you are the "angels" God has given care over those who sleep.

We tend to think that angels are something like fairies, only bigger, whiter, and with larger feathered wings. One of the Old Testament stories about angels is that of Jacob who sees the angels going up and down a ladder between heaven and earth. In Hebrew the word for angel means messenger or agent. There are messengers and agents of grace transacting the work of the Creator. That is often how I think of you. You are agents of Grace easing pain, offering comfort, ever caring for those who suffer, and sustaining the dignity of those passing from life to death.

You may never think of it that way. Or you may not believe in angels or certainly do not think of yourself as one. But that's OK. I have long been convinced that there are "angels unaware." They are people just like you who imagine that you are only doing your job changing diapers, administering pain medication, serving food, cleaning up vomit, or bathing a patient.

Angels unaware may not be cute like "Daddy's little angel" that you see on the shirt of a toddler. Angels unaware may have personal idiosyncrasies that drive the rest of us crazy, are sometimes self-destructive, and certainly have their share of issues. But none of that stops them from doing the work of compassion, the essential ingredient of God's grace. I thank you for all of that and it is my privilege to see it every day.

Now, LISTEN UP, I am here for you. Yes, you.
Your Chaplain,
Gary

The Chaplain's Chart – for the Week of July 1, 2013

"Scintillate, scintillate, globule vivific, Fain would I fathom thy nature specific. Loftily poised in the ether capacious, Strongly resembling a gem carbonaceous."
How would you translate these lines? I'll tell you the correct answer further down in the column.

Communication is a vital sign of any healthy organization, but most especially a hospital. Imagine a surgical suite with the best medical equipment money can buy, the highest skilled surgeons and anesthetists, and the most competent surgical nurses. The one thing they lack is communication. The surgeon holds out his hand but says nothing. How does the nurse know what instrument he wants, or size and gauge? It would not work, would it? There is no transaction in this hospital that can be accomplished without clear communication and a shared understanding of our common language.

This can be pretty tricky business. Consider the story of Neil Marten, a member of the British Parliament. He was once giving a tour of the House of Commons for his constituents. During the tour the group encountered Lord Hailsham, Lord Chancellor. He was wearing all of the robes and regalia of his high office. Hailsham recognized Marten and called out, "Neil." Not daring to disobey the Lord Chancellor, the touring group promptly fell to its knees.

This is an ever-present challenge, even for God. Trying to convince his people that what God really expected of them was not elaborate and ornate rituals and sacrifices. No, we hear his voice in Micah (6:8), "He has showed you, O man, what is good. And what does the Lord require of you? To act justly, and to love mercy and to walk humbly with your God." But not everyone heard that or got the message, thus requiring of God a more blunt statement as is found in Amos (5:21): "I hate, I despise your religious feasts; I cannot stand your assemblies...Away with the noise of your songs!...But let justice roll on like a river, righteousness like a never-failing stream." Is it clear now?

Communication is about clarity of thoughts, plans, and actions. Who will be affected by these plans and how quickly can they be brought into the conversation? Every organization has a mission statement with goals and strategies to implement that mission. But if these are not articulated on a daily basis they have little relevance to the business of the organization. When we are not communicating throughout the hospital our work becomes ineffective, our relationships are crippled, people feel disempowered, and then other forms of communication arise – gossip and rumor.

And here is how the opening lines of this meditation are best translated:

Twinkle, twinkle little star, How I wonder what you are.

Up above the world so high, Like a diamond in the sky.

So, let's talk.

I am hear for you. (Pun intended.)

Your Chaplain,

Gary

The Chaplain's Chart – for the Week of July 8, 2013

This past weekend a passenger jet crash-landed in San Francisco, killing two people, with close to two hundred injured. A plane crashed in Alaska, killing all ten passengers aboard. A train freighting oil derailed in Quebec. According to all reports the train was stopped and properly braked for the mandatory rest of the engineer. For whatever reason the brakes slipped and the train started rolling into the town of Lac-Megantic where it careened off the tracks. Fierce explosions and fire destroyed much of the town. Five people are known dead, and 40 are missing. Some speculate that victims may have been "vaporized" by the heat of burning oil and ether.

Friday evening I was officiating at a wedding in El Dorado's East Park. Right before the ceremony began I saw an ambulance and the water rescue unit rushing toward the lake. Later I learned that a man had drowned. His wife and three children were anxiously waiting at lakeside for the hopeful recovery of the husband and father. I thought of the paradox of one family celebrating a wedding while at the same time in the same town another grieved the death of a loved one.

During such events I often hear people ask, "Why did God let this happen?" or "Why doesn't God stop this?" People often think that all of these events were the will of God, which suggests that God caused it all to happen. Language gets blurred and people think that evil suffering has been intentionally inflicted on others.

I do not believe that. Disease, trauma, old age, and death are part of what it means to be a human being. In all of the situations

I have mentioned above there were natural forces, such as physics, involved. God did not plan or will that Oscar Rodriguez Vargas drown in El Dorado Lake. Mr. Vargas was not wearing a life jacket despite the entreaties of his friends to do so. He could not swim well. He had good intentions in his heart, retrieving the boat of his friend. But he went out beyond his means and slipped into the 119 foot drop-off. At that point all of the powers of nature and biology set in motion the drowning of Mr. Vargas. There was no moral evil at work here. This was not the handiwork of God.

But God's will was certainly at work that afternoon. The water rescue team labored relentlessly for two hours. Family and friends wept and prayed. They will gather together and memorialize husband and father. And I pray that we will see God's hand working in the years ahead to nourish and sustain his widow and children.

For me the question is not "What is God up to now?" or "Why is God doing this to us?" The question I have to ask is that regardless of what is happening now, am I doing God's will? Am I loving my neighbor as myself? Is my spirit drenched with God's love, forgiveness, kindness, and mercy? In moments of suffering or terror I can only pray with John Henry Newman:

> Lead, kindly Light, amid the encircling gloom,
> Lead Thou me on!
> The night is dark, and I am far from home;
> Lead Thou me on!
> Keep Thou my feet; I do not ask to see
> The distant scene, one step enough for me.

Remember that I am your chaplain too,
Gary

Did you know that the first requirement – expectation – hope for any chaplain is to show up? That is true for any minister, priest, rabbi, or imam I know of. Each of these religious leaders might read from different scriptures, offer prayers in unique languages, or tender rituals and sacraments that are distinctively their own. But none of that matters if they do not show up. The presence of spiritual leaders plays a very important social role.

An increasing body of evidence shows the relationship between the progression of disease and loneliness. Dr. John Cacioppo of the University of Chicago studies the biological effect of loneliness. He and other researchers such as Steve Cole of UCLA have demonstrated that diseases such as heart disease are exacerbated by loneliness. There is a physiological change in body chemistry that raises mortality rates among lonely patients.

Loneliness is not resolved with social media such as Twitter, Facebook, or email. I am talking about the physical presence of other human beings who take the time to chat with us, catch up on news from home, gossip about people at church, and gently ease the conversation into deeper conversations about well being. It concerns me that so many patients in hospitals like ours, or nursing homes, or mental health inpatient facilities, are never visited by friends, family, or churches.

My spiritual director reminded me last week that it is not only the "chaplain" that calls on a patient, parishioner, member of the family, or a friend. When a patient asks for the chaplain, he or she is hoping for a Sacred encounter. They are anticipating that no one less than the Author of Life knocks on their door. Or to put it another way, it's not about me. It is about the presence of God, meeting with them as they encounter pain, surgery, catastrophic disease, or comfort care for the end of their days.

A careful reading of the Psalms reveals the plea of common people like us for the presence of God in our pain, suffering, isolation, death, and national catastrophe.

One example is Psalm 116:1-4:

I love the Lord, because he had heard
my voice and my supplications.
Because he inclined his ear to me,
therefore I will call on him as long as I live.
The snare of death encompassed me;
I suffered distress and anguish.
Then I called on the name of the Lord:
"O Lord, I pray, save my life."

This is just one of many examples. The Psalms reach across the major Western religions of Christianity, Judaism, and Islam. Aside from the fact that these three religions share this Biblical heritage, the Psalms speak to the soul of humanity that few other poems and hymns are able to do. The fundamental question they ask is, "God, where are you in my distress?" The fundamental answer from the psalmist is, "I am continually with you; you hold my right hand, you guide me with your counsel, and afterward you receive me with honor." (73:24)

Did you know that in Chinese society eating alone is unthought-of? Authentic Chinese restaurants are peopled with family and friends. A large lazy Susan in the center of the table contains multiple dishes that the whole company is served from. Likewise, no one should suffer alone or die alone. We should all show up.

You do not have to be alone either. I hope you know that I am here for you.

Your Chaplain,
Gary

The Chaplain's Chart – for the Week of July 22, 2013

Albert Schweitzer, Mother Theresa, Dorothy Day, Dr. Martin Luther King Jr., Clara Barton, The Mahatma Gandhi, Dorothea Dix, Helen Keller, Buddha, and Jesus of Nazareth represent a small group of people who had one thing in common. Can you guess what it is? They do not all share the same gender, ethnicity, race, or creed. What they all share is the understanding that we are only healed when we engage the suffering of disease, or injustice, or trauma. Each in his or her own way tried to diagnose the problem, offer therapeutic alternatives, and follow the protocols. Only when we dance with suffering can we transform it.

But I think it goes deeper than that. It is only when we embrace human suffering that we fully encounter the presence of God. Yes, I see God in the faces of children, on mountain tops, beside the roaring sea, and drinking a fine cup of coffee in the morning while I read Emily Dickinson. But I have not fully plumbed the depths of God if I refuse to wade into the room of a screaming six-year-old who has pulled out her IV line or an alcoholic who nearly drank himself to death and probably will not seek rehabilitation. To take the pulse of God means that I listen to the stories of the hungry and homeless, feeding and sheltering them when I can.

Jesus had another way of phrasing the question. In Matthew's gospel (20:20-28) the mother of the Zebedee boys asked Jesus if her sons could sit beside his throne, one on the right and one on the left. Jesus tells her that she does not know what she is asking and then poses this question, "Can you drink the cup I am going to drink?" He goes on to say that if you want to sit by Jesus you must make yourself the servant of all – to be the servant of every need, hurt, joy, pain, disappointment, thrill, tear, gasp, laugh, smile, and stark terror. Can you drink that cup? The whole cup?

One of my favorite spiritual authors is Henri Nouwen. He was celebrating the Eucharist at Daybreak, a residential treatment facility for people who were mentally or developmentally challenged. In this small company of about 20 people he had a remarkable insight about this tiny community and the meaning of Holy Communion. In his book, *Can You Drink the Cup,* Father Nouwen wrote, "Can you drink the cup? Can you empty it to the dregs? Can you live your life to the full, whatever it will bring?"

We cannot be authentically human unless we drink the whole cup. We cannot be at home with God unless we drink the cup with all of its joys and sorrows.

60

What we do in a hospital is share the cup of life. And drink the whole cup we must if there is to be hope and healing.

Remember that if you are looking for a drinking partner, I am here for you!

Your Chaplain,

Gary

The Chaplain's Chart – for the Week of August 5, 2013

Someone once remarked that we cannot play a violin if the strings are not stretched. The same is true for our lives. We imagine that we would like to just "hang loose," relax, and fully inhale the aroma of life. I think that is necessary but I do not think that is how we live our lives on a day-to-day basis. There has to be some tension in our lives if we want to make music. We have to be stretched and pulled and challenged if we really want to grow.

I am not saying that we should be stretched so tight that the strings break. That can happen and it is not really healthy. But if we just slouch around we are not likely to be effective or creative. There are people, of course, who protest when they are required to extend themselves beyond the normal. They resent change, the pressure to learn new techniques and skills, and the rising levels of expectation. Such people often find themselves in unemployment lines and searching online dating services.

A healthy life is about the constant process of tuning, keeping the right tension on the strings of our lives. Stringed instruments have to be tuned every day, and sometimes after every song. It is true for violins, bodies, relationships, and work. It is also true for our souls.

I think we have missed the boat if we think that tuning our souls means that we go to church, mosque, or synagogue every week, say grace before every meal, and read the Bible every day with time for prayer and meditation. Don't get me wrong, those are important disciplines. But such habits do not make everything go smoothly. Part of tuning the soul is asking yourself what feels wrong. Why am I so angry? Why do I feel so put upon? Why does this or that threaten me? Whenever I feel these emotions I have learned to ask, "What is God challenging me to do/know/understand now?" What is that rascally Creator up to, and what is it that I need to be learning?

More often than not God does not take me out for ice cream when I need to learn something to grow. I am sure I am the problem. I am a slow learner. So God allows me to bump into things, fall down, and take a kick in the pants. It is sort of like riding a horse. It is never a question of if you are going to fall off, but when. That is how we learn and become skilled riders. We could protest, blame the horse, and say riding a horse is not fair. But the accomplished equestrian gets back in the saddle and says to his or her mount, "Walk on." Wouldn't you know that "horse training" should really be called "rider training." And because of my own recalcitrance God is constantly taking me back to the round pen to work on one more soul skill.

Going back to the metaphor of the violin, God is a patient musician who is constantly tuning me. God knows I squeal, squawk, and scratch at every pull of the bow. I am learning that prayer life is not the repetition of holy words. It is the constant turning of the pegs of grace that stretches me. And guess who turns the pegs?

Never forget that I am here for you.

Gary

The Chaplain's Chart – for the Week of August 12, 2013

Robert Carr wrote in *The Center*:

Could it be that my aching for the anguish of the world
Is the feeling of my heart being enlarged?
Could it be that my willingness to ache
For my suffering neighbor
Is my purest assent to God's perfect intent?

We often hear people use the phrase, "It just breaks my heart," to describe a personal or family tragedy. Or you will hear them say, "The pain in my heart is too much to bear." Without a doubt our hearts ache and we feel real pain in our chest. Our minds and souls are burdened by a grief that often seems unsustainable.

Robert Carr invites us to consider the possibility that the pain we feel is also the ache of a heart "being enlarged." The heart is a muscle, of course, and I am reminded of childhood "growing pains" where the child feels discomfort as his or her body grows and stretches. This occurs in 25% to 40% of children, usually following a day of athletic exercises. The pain will sometimes wake them in the night and they respond well to gentle massage.

To follow the metaphor, when we enter the suffering of other human beings our hearts – or souls – get exercised, perhaps even fatigued. But I submit to you that this indicates a growing muscle, an expanding capacity to receive the needs of others and bless them with compassion.

Why is this important? We cannot stand it if our hearts only get broken and all we experience is the trauma of another person; if we are only shocked at the ravages of disease; or if we are only stunned by the death of a human being. We would be wise to mechanically go through the motions of stanching the wound, pushing the fluids or meds, and finally cleaning the body of the deceased. No need to get emotionally and spiritually involved if the only result is pain in our hearts. Haven't we got enough of that in our own lives already? Why risk emotional breakdown?

But if the willingness to ache for the suffering of our neighbors means entering the presence and love of God's will for us, growing pains become a real gift. We will not be so eager to block the anguish of others when we understand that suffering is God's operating theater. And the deeper we enter Sacred Suffering our hearts grow stronger, our faith deepens, and we learn to meet joy on the other side of despair.

I remain Your Chaplain,
Gary

The late Bishop Charles L. Slattery of the Episcopal Diocese of Massachusetts wrote about the reality and necessity of opposites. He wrote, "There is always a note of pathos in the most joyous music; tears are always locked in the happiest smiles; the poems of dramas of love which reveal the highest bliss always include tragedy."

Yes, there are seeming opposites in the world: light and dark, fast and slow, life and death, black and white, pleasure and pain, joy and sorrow. Our knowledge of opposites, however, only identifies the extreme ranges of life, but seldom do we live there. We live in some melding of the opposites. Sometimes it is not opposites that have blended together but a whole range of feelings that cannot be adequately named or defined. For example, when a loved one dies we may feel great sorrow, a sense of relief, hope for life to come, and a smudge of guilt about what else we might have done for the dearly departed. These feelings may press upon our hearts all at once. Or each feeling pummels us in rapid succession. Or they jump out at you in the most unexpected times and places.

My daughter, Emily, started high school last week. I don't mind telling you that I felt great anxiety for her. There was also a sad and hopeful recognition that she is growing up and this is an important step in her future. And yes, I worried about boys – a lot. It's not that I don't trust Emily, but I do not trust boys. I was one once and have a pretty good idea what they are thinking about most of the time.

The same is true for our souls, the centre of our being. Faith is often the partner of doubt, hope is fatigued by distrust, vision is blurred by the power of evil, and righteousness is always tempted by selfish greed. Even St. Paul struggled with this as we see from his letter to the Romans, "I do not understand my own actions. For I do not do what I want, but I do the very thing I hate." (7:15) Paul understands that his faith does not depend on eliminating the contradictions or tensions in his life. Faith surrenders the opposites to the grace of God. Or parts of them, I think.

We live with this blend of opposites and tensions everyday here at the hospital. This is true for every medical procedure, patient interaction, and the relationships we have with each other. We are a rural hospital in a small town where we see each other or our patients at Wal-Mart or the high school football game. We sometimes treat our neighbors or our teacher from elementary school. All of this is fraught with the pull of opposites and that great big gray arena we call life. The challenge is for us to embrace this life as if it were the Garden of Eden; because it is the only garden that God has given us.

These words from my favorite writer, Author Unknown:

> They tell me I must bruise the rose's leaf,
> Ere I can keep and use its fragrance brief.
> They tell me I must break the skylark's heart,
> Ere cage song will make the silent start.
> They tell me love must bleed and friendship weep
> Ere my sorest need I touch that deep.
> Must it be always so with precious things,
> Must they be bruised, and go with beaten wings?
> Ah, yes! by crushing days, by caging nights, by scar
> Of thorns and stony ways, these blessings are.

Your Chaplain,
Gary

The Chaplain's Chart – for the Week of August 26, 2013

I was fifteen years old when Dr. Martin Luther King, Jr. spoke at the March on Washington for Jobs and Freedom. We know that famous oratory as the "I Have a Dream Speech." Most of Dr. King's speech was written though he embellished it with some asides. At the end of his prepared remarks the great "Queen of Gospel" singer, Mahalia Jackson shouted to Dr. King, "Tell them about the dream, Martin." And he did, with this preface, "I have a dream that one day this nation will rise up and live out the true meaning of its creed, 'We hold these truths to be self-evident, that all men are created equal.'" Perhaps the most quoted part of the speech is, "I have a dream that my four little children will one day live in a nation where they will not be judged by the color of their skin but by the content of their character."

Like most Southerners I grew up with a great deal of prejudice. When I have the occasion to speak with teenagers about this period of American history I report that African Americans were not allowed into "white" restaurants and had to pick up their food at the back door of the kitchen; were not allowed to swim in public pools; were not allowed to drink from the same water fountains or use the same public rest rooms. Black children were educated in separate and very unequal schools. More than anything they were not allowed to vote. I witnessed these and other atrocities, but today's teenagers do not believe me. They think I am making it up until they are shown the films and photographs.

The Civil Rights movement was very threatening to most Americans, especially in the South. It was not just the challenge to voter rights and segregation. The Civil Rights movement held up the entire culture of prejudice, fear, and discrimination – our way of life – and found it disgraceful. Nobody wanted to know that their social mores and "way of doing things" was immoral. We hated to hear it and the men who brought that prophetic voice, especially Malcolm X.

The problem with Dr. King was he was a great preacher. Southerners love great preaching and we could not escape the truth and power of his rhetoric. I sometimes tell people that Dr. King saved my soul. He preached the gospel truth with the power of the Old Testament prophets and I was "convicted" of the sin of prejudice. He won me over to the truth of human dignity, equality, and that dream of character without regard to skin color or any other difference.

Everyone knows that we have seen great strides in race relations since 1963. The march on Washington is often credited with the passage of the Civil Rights Act of 1964 and the Voting Rights Act of 1965. But the American soul continues to be stained with prejudices of every stripe. This includes, of course, color but also gender, gender orientation, religious identities like Jews and Muslims, age and ability, economic and social class, nationality and ethnicity. There is much work to do. It reminds me of the lyrics of English poet John Donne (1572-1631), "No Man Is an Island:"

No man is an island
No man stands alone.
Each man's joy is joy to me,
Each man's grief is my own.

We need one another,
So I will defend,
Each man as my brother,
Each man as my friend

I belong to each of you, my brothers and sisters. And as Donne would conclude his poem, "When I help my brother and sister, then I know that I plant the seed of friendship that will never die." Or in the words of Dr. King, that is when we will all know that we are "free at last."

Your Chaplain,
Gary

The Chaplain's Chart – for the Week of October 7, 2013

I enjoyed my trip to Florida. The wedding went well and I got to visit with family whom I have not seen in a few years. Saturday afternoon I went sailing with my brother on his boat, *Lucille.* There was a light wind and we did not go much faster than three knots. I enjoyed the sights of osprey, sea turtles, brown pelicans, and bottle-nosed dolphins. We shared fresh caught grouper, raw oysters on the half-shell, seafood gumbo, alligator tail, and key lime pie. There were only a few snags with the family crazies but that's not bad for a wedding weekend. There is a lot here to be thankful for and I truly am.

Saturday morning my daughter, Heather, took me up to All Children's Hospital in St. Petersburg to visit her stepdaughter's four-month-old. He was born with significant heart issues and will require open-heart surgery when he is bigger and able to withstand it.

Right after he was born a shunt had to be placed in his heart, which collapsed a week ago last Sunday, or so we were told. Talking with the cardiac intensive care nurse she said that the shunt had filled with coagulated blood, which threw him into a crisis. By the way, she observed, there is a slight brain bleed but that seems to have stopped. He is on a ventilator and feeding tube, which they had hoped to remove last Thursday, but the tissue surrounding it is so swollen they fear extubation will tear the swollen tissue. If the medication he was given to stop the swelling fails they will remove it surgically today.

The boy's name is George. He was alert and followed me with his eyes. Heather and I talked with him but were not able to hold him. I offered him a blessing and made the sign of the cross on his forehead. Sometimes he seemed to smile. There is no way to determine if he suffered any brain damage as a result of not breathing when he went into crisis. I do not know how long he was down. But all of his blood chemistry and gases were good as of Saturday. There is a lot here to be thankful for and I truly am.

We tend to think that goodness and blessing can only be found in weddings, good food, and a joyous family. I experienced a lot of goodness and blessing this past weekend. But blessing and goodness follow us even into pediatric intensive care units. George had the blessing of wonderfully skilled emergency technicians, doctors, and nurses. He has a family who loves him and dares to pray for his wholeness. He has a family who dares to hope even when the odds are against him. And if George dies we will weep but one day we will remember the child who followed us with his eyes.

Occasionally people ask me to pray for their loved ones. Sometimes they stop by my office and say something directly, or mention them in a hallway passing, or send me an email. There are some explanations given but also only a name. Every week I start a new list. May I ask you to pray for George this week? And by all means share your prayer concerns with me as well. As you might expect these are always kept confidential.

I am still here for you, and I remain,
Your Chaplain,
Gary

We work in a world of high expectations, and there are none higher than in a hospital where the expectations are of perfection. People come to us who are ill, injured, and may be dying. They expect their food to taste just like momma's back home. They honestly think that pain management is the same thing as complete freedom from pain. They never imagine that surgical procedures will result in anything but full recovery, despite all of the liability forms they sign.

We expect perfection of ourselves. We feel bad when a pain riddled patient blows up at us, as if we were the cause of their pain. We blame ourselves when patients die. We feel bad/angry/guilty/humiliated when a procedure gets fouled up or we chart the wrong information. Much of our work requires precision and we strive for perfection.

No one can doubt the importance of competent medical care. We expect exactitude from the surgeon's scalpel and the pharmacist's measure. People are paid to insure compliance with HIPAA while others review charts and charges for accuracy. Patient satisfaction scores are constantly before us.

All of this is absolutely necessary and it will not be any other way. But I hope that does not delude us into the thinking that human perfection is finally possible or that mistakes will never be made. Even when we are as perfect as perfect can be cancer cells grow, people die, and someone slips on the wet floor of the dish room. Even when we bring state of the art medical services to people they are finally given health by the grace of God. We helped, but life is always a matter of God's providence.

When we forget the limits of human perfection or perfectibility we set ourselves up for bitter disappointment. The idea that we can heal everyone verges on the kind of pride that brings us all down. Somewhere in the deeper reaches of God's mystery are life and abundance, death and limitation.

One of the most fascinating books of the Hebrew Bible is Job. Within the very first chapter we learn that he is a righteous man – as good as we get. Messengers come to him and inform him that his crops and herds have been destroyed or rustled. Then comes the news that strong winds knocked down the house where all of his children were feasting and were all killed. What is Job's response? He goes into mourning and worships God saying, "Naked came I out of my mother's womb, and naked shall I return thither: the Lord gave, and the Lord hath taken away; blessed be the name of the Lord." That line has found its way into many graveside rituals.

Despite all of our skills and every effort at perfection the power of life and death is not ultimately ours to hold. For that reason I pray that my life be directed by and empowered by grace, not perfection. I have seen many resuscitations in my life but I know that not one of them was a resurrection. It is essential to my humanity, my sanity, and my faith to know the difference.

I know you well enough to understand that you will keep honing your skills and striving to perfection. I love you well enough to encourage you to grace. After all, I am here for you only by the grace of God.

Your Chaplain,
Gary

The Chaplain's Chart – for the Week of November 11, 2013

Whenever we think about sickness and illness we must first understand that we are discussing a community. The body is a community of cells, tissues, organs, and bones. Think about a single drop of blood. It is a community of red cells, white cells, leukocytes, and platelets. That community is suspended in another community we call plasma, which contains water, proteins, mineral ions, hormones, and carbon dioxide. The body is a community of communities. Sickness, disease, or trauma is a disruption in the life of the community. Community relations are broken and we call it cancer, or measles, or a broken bone.

Modern physicists like Einstein, Plank, Bohr, and Heisenberg attest to the fact that all matter is relational. There is nothing in this universe that is a single isolated bit of matter, even if we talk about subatomic particles. Everything is relational and it seems to be the nature of matter to attract and bond to other bits of matter to create a new community we call cells, minerals, plants, or animals.

So when we "treat" a patient we are not simply treating an infection, broken bone, or diseased organ. We are treating a community we call a patient. But don't stop there. The patient's community is physical, and also mental, and spiritual. We know there is a clear and unmistakable relationship between mental and spiritual health and physical recovery. If we think we only enter a patient's room to administer a medication or breathing treatment and not care for the whole person we do not understand healing. Healing is a relationship that ministers to the whole patient.

But don't stop there. When a patient enters Susan B. Allen he or she brings his or her whole family, friends, co-workers, and faith community. The patient's community of communities also plays an important role in the restoration of health. We have also seen the sad impact of patients who are alone and isolated or whose families are actually detrimental to their health. I have seen patients die but I know their families will be whole and they will be healthy because of the depth and breadth of their love, support, and humor. I have also seen families whose grief will be bitter because their "community" is abrasive and angry. South African and Zulu poet, Mzwakhe Mubli wrote:

> An injury to the head,
> Is an injury to the whole person,
> Is an injury to the whole family,
> Is an injury to the compound,
> Is an injury to the village,
> Is an injury to the kingdom,
> Is an injury to the world.

So what has all of that got to do with your work at S.B.A. Memorial Hospital? Good medicine treats the whole person and every one of us can take a little bit of time to listen, console, and comfort. Listen to their stories, read their faces, watch their body language and never be afraid to wish them "Godspeed," or "Be at peace my friend," or "Bless you." I have no territorial claims on such language. That is the language of community and it is meant for all of us to share. And please don't forget that I am here for you, too.

Your Chaplain,
Gary

The Chaplain's Chart – for the Week of November 18, 2013

Several years ago we were getting ready for church. The kids were in the back seat. I backed the car out of the garage and waited for my wife, Mimi, to come out of the house. I could see the back door through my rear view mirror. I saw Mimi coming out and lock the door. Glancing away for only a few seconds I looked back in the mirror and Mimi had disappeared. I thought she had gone back into the house. After a couple of minutes she did not come out of the door so I honked the horn. Still, no Mimi. In exasperation I got out of the car to get her.

When I got out of the car, there was Mimi lying on the ground, face up. Her leg was resting on the steps. She was laughing but she could not stand up. She was wearing a pair of those old granny boots with long shoelaces, which she had not tied. One got caught in the door as she closed it, pulled tight and down she went. The tension was so great that she could not figure out how to stand up. We still laugh about that story.

Why is it that the little things trip us up? We can birth hundreds of babies but often remember the one that died. We perform a thousand surgeries successfully but ruminate on the ones that went wrong. Wracking our brains we keep processing the whole event trying to find out what we did wrong. What did we miss? What did we overlook? What was the tiny detail that set the dominoes of death in motion?

We have often heard, "Don't sweat the small stuff." The problem is that just about everything is made up of small stuff. Leave the baking powder out of your biscuit recipe and you've got a hockey puck. The pin on a hand grenade is pretty small compared to the whole. Lose it and the consequences can be devastating.

At the same time it is the small stuff that often brings us great joy and comfort. Yesterday after the Sunday service eighteen-month-old Addie came up to me and took my hand. I picked her up and she immediately laid her head on my shoulder. Addie stayed there about 15 minutes. It was a blessing from a small child. Saturday I was alone in our country home. I went out on the front porch and sat down on the bench. Drinking a hot cup of PG Tips (an English tea) I absorbed the warm sun while the wind raced across the prairie. It was a simple ritual of solace.

As fall tumbles into winter think about the small things. Keep your eyes open for little shifts that scamper across the field, like the subtle change of color that comes from the wintering sun on orange leaves. Watch for mice that scurry into small holes in your house for their season of offspring. Pay attention to the lone snowflake that blows in the high beams of your headlights. Linger over the aroma of hot coffee and pumpkin bread. Let them climb up on your shoulders to rest and bless you.

I am your chaplain,
Gary

The Chaplain's Chart – for the Week of December 2, 2013

Yesterday the Christian church celebrated the first Sunday in Advent. It is actually the first day, or New Year's Day, of the Christian calendar. Advent is the season of expectation as our eyes turn east searching for a bright star that leads to the manger. We light the first candle of the Advent wreath to prepare our hearts to receive the gift of grace. Advent is the waiting room of Christ's Mass, or Christmas.

We could quickly identify waiting rooms at our hospital. There is, of course, the lobby where people wait for the admission process to begin; waiting rooms for the emergency department, lab, cancer treatment center, radiology, OB-GYN, and dialysis. But when you think about it every room in the hospital is a waiting room. People are waiting for test results, a baby to be born, a procedure, a surgery, physical therapy, and a discharge home. There is always hope and expectation for the lab work to be negative for cancer, a healthy baby girl or boy, and a mended bone. Patients wait for balance and regular bowels, the twin passports of dismissal.

Waiting is sometimes very difficult. Waiting is the place where hope and fear pace around in our minds and neither one of them is willing to sit down and read the two year old copy of *Field and Stream* magazine. Waiting is difficult because our imaginations can conjure the worst possible outcomes, the changes we will have to make, and the cost of treatment and recovery. Waiting is the possibility of walking without our knees buckling, sight that is no longer clouded by cataracts, or restored life with a heart catheterization and stents. Hope and fear, expectation and uncertainty, love and joy in the presence of death are the characteristics of Advent.

I love to sing the Advent hymn, "O Come, O Come, Emmanuel." It is an antiphon, meaning that the priest or liturgist sings a line and the congregation responds. If you read the lyrics carefully you will see both the tension and the hope of Advent.

> O come, O come, Emmanuel!
> And ransom captive Israel
> That mourns in lonely exile here
> Until the Son of God appear.
> Rejoice! Rejoice! Emmanuel
> Shall come to thee, O Israel.

Do you see what is at stake in Advent? Do you see the light that defies the tyranny of exile, loneliness, and grief? That is our playing field. Everyday is Advent at the hospital, no matter the diagnosis or prognosis. So, light your candles, rejoice when possible, and keep hope alive.

On a personal note, it is possible that my great grandson, George, will be home by Christmas. During his open-heart surgery they closed four holes and put in place a pulmonary stent.

I hope you know that all of you have a place in my heart. Never worry that it is too crowded. There is always room for you.

I am your Chaplain, *Gary*

A fourth grader I know of comes from a deeply conflicted family. I think he must be afflicted with some anxiety disorder. At eight o'clock in the morning he paces outside the elementary school, trying to gather up enough strength to walk through the doors. Finally he musters enough fortitude to enter the building, but he does not go to his classroom. He slips into the counselor's office and curls up on an overstuffed chair. He spends an hour or so with her. She seeks to reassure him. The boy then moves to the principal's office who tries to bring comfort and courage to the boy. It is not until 11:00 that the boy makes it into the classroom. For a few hours he is freed from his anxiety.

This happens every day.

The counselor, principle, teacher and classroom aides would probably tell you, "I'm only doing my job."

I believe it is more than that. I believe that this boy and these educators are creating a sacred moment. They are establishing a holy communion where fear and chaos are shut out and a little boy has a chance at freedom and hope. This is the essence of a "God Moment."

In her book, *Practical Mysticism,* Evelyn Underhill helps us understand that we cannot know God in isolation. She wrote, "We know a thing only by uniting with it; by assimilating it; by an interpenetration of it and ourselves." When that happens, Reality, in both its material and spiritual manifestation, produces a Holy Encounter.

Now I would be willing to bet that these educators are not conscious of their ministry. They would probably speak the language of educational psychology, or behavioral modification, or best practices in school discipline. Yes, it is all of that. But it is also the fact that they are uniting with and assimilating this child in their hearts and minds. There is an interpenetration of compassion and suffering, professionalism and hope, a frightened child and caring adults. In my mind there is an Unseen Visitor in this school blessing a child whose family home is chaotic.

And guess what? I see this sacred activity at Susan B.

Allen Memorial Hospital every day. When you assimilate the needs of patients and fellow workers into quality medical care and compassion you are doing holy work. Even when all you can offer is "comfort care," and if you do it with kindness and empathy, you are integrating your entire being with the life of that patient and his or her family. That is Holy Stuff.

St. Paul declared that God is not far from each one of us. "For in Him we live and move and have our being." (Acts 17:28). For us that means that God is with the surgeon's scalpel, the physical therapist's guiding hand, the pharmacist's careful measure, and the providence of the baker's bread. Everything that happens in this hospital occurs in the presence of the Creator, Sustainer, and Redeemer of life – and all lives.

God's presence among us is constant. Paul wrote to the Romans that there is nothing that can separate us from the love of God. My challenge is to open my eyes and ears to know that presence and love in everything that we do here.

With such love I am here for you.

Gary

The Chaplain's Chart – for the Week of January 20, 2014

Last April, I adopted a rescue horse, Sapphire. She was brought to the rescue facility severely underweight. They were able to get some weight back on her and we are still working to get weight on her haunches, back, and muscles on her neck and shoulders. If I cannot do this we will not be able to ride her.

The first thing I do about 5:45 in the morning is put on the coffee. I then head out to feed the horses. Sapphire gets senior feed with a cup of alfalfa pellets. I feed her twice a day, and close the gate to the arena to keep out the goats, donkeys, and the other horse. All of them try to get into each other's food. Heck, even my dogs will eat horse food. Sapphire also gets MSM, a powder that I put in her food for joint relief.

Of course the veterinarian has looked at her and we keep a careful eye out for worms. We also have her teeth "floated," which means they are ground to be even. Sapphire has lost a lot of her teeth, which is why it takes such a long time for her to eat. The farrier comes about every six weeks to trim the hoofs of our donkeys and horses. When it starts getting warmer and lighter in the evenings I will start working the horses in the round pen to build muscle strength.

Most of the animals that we love and care for have been abandoned in one way or another. One of our goats was a "runt," though to look at her today you would think she is pregnant with three kids. The other is a Nubian goat that is way past milking. Our duck, "Rosie," was brought to us by my daughter's school friend, who had gotten her for Easter. Rosie wore out cute for this friend, though I enjoy talking with Rosie. She is quite funny. Emily's horse is a wonderfully trained American Quarter Horse who was over ridden as a working cow horse in South Dakota. He is a perfect horse for a young person but cannot carry too much weight over long distances. And then there is Yevette, the Christmas goose who was given to us for dinner. She is alive and well and we have long conversations whenever I feed the chickens. Yevette lets me stroke her breast. Her eyes are as blue as the skies of Kansas.

We could easily change the characters of this little romp to describe a member of our family or a patient in our hospital. In the love and care of them we might include the services of primary care doctors, dieticians, physical therapists, podiatrists, and geriatric specialists. Increasing numbers of vets today utilize massage therapy and acupuncture in the care of horses.

In either scenario we are talking about tremendous amounts of money. Our horses eat about 100 pounds of horse feed a week, at a cost of nearly $40.00.

So why do we do this? Why do we spend so much money, time, and energy for these creatures, equine and human? The all too easy answer is "love." Yes, it is that, but far deeper and more profound. What if I said it is a love that exploded with the gas and stardust of the creation? What if the power of creation constantly moves life and lives forward, totally unconcerned with the costs or the time it takes?

Somebody might say to me, "All of this time and money you are spending on horses is absurd." Or, "When you retire you are going to be sorry that you did not put more money into your retirement account and spent less money on your animals." You could say that about all of the time and money we spend on our daughter's dance lessons, shoes, and costumes. But the answer is that this Divine Impetus is always oriented to the creation, redemption, and sustenance of life and its future. It propels me to care for the living, regardless of their age and stage in life.

Your Chaplain,
Gary

The Chaplain's Chart – for the Week of January 27, 2014

Emily Dickinson wrote:

> Surgeons must be very careful
> When they take the knife!
> Underneath their fine incisions
> Stirs the Culprit – Life!

Emily clearly respects the skill of surgical medicine. She notes "fine incisions" and not cutting or slicing. One can imagine the delicate work that hardly leaves a scar. Yet for all of the delicacy of their skill, there lies beneath the patient's skin a culprit. The culprit is no less than life itself.

Culprit is an interesting word. The first syllable is *cul*, from the Latin, meaning guilty or responsible. *Prit* is from the Anglo-French meaning ready. Imagine an English court scene in the seventeenth century when a prisoner stands before the bar in criminal court. In American law this would be a time of arraignment and plea entry. The Clerk of the Crown asks, "Culprit, how will you be tried?" The prisoner might respond, "Not guilty." The Clerk insists, "You are guilty. We are ready to prove our indictment."

Emily understands that despite the surgeon's skill and careful work, it is life that is finally responsible for the outcome of the surgery. We are not, of course, talking about gross negligence or ineptitude on the part of the doctor. We are talking about the ultimate fact that it is life itself that determines the outcomes of all of our best skills and talents. Hopefully the result of the surgery will be recovery and good health. But courtrooms are packed with cases where the best surgical arts resulted in severe disabilities or death. There is no medical explanation of why this happens.

Emily notes that the Culprit stirs. Life is mixing things up with the surgeon. He or she is not a lone actor in the surgical theatre. There is always another player who does not necessarily follow the script, medical protocols, and hospital policy. Life seems to prefer improvisation and the riffing of a jazz musician rather than the strict musical notation of a classical score.

All of us know the wisdom of Emily Dickinson's poem. Who has not laid out, planted, fertilized, weeded, and watered a garden only to find it destroyed by insects or a drought that is more powerful than soaker hoses? Or have you ever followed a recipe to the letter and watched the cake collapse or the pie turn bitter? A friend of mine spent nearly forty years in the ministry. Russ was a good pastor and a tireless agent of social justice. He looked forward to his retirement with plans to travel and enjoy some adult education classes. But within a year of his retirement he was diagnosed with cancer and died after months of pain and suffering.

Life stirs and some of the dumbest things we ever do become expressions of beauty or goodness. Some of the tastiest vegetables I ever grew were "volunteers" that popped up out of the compost heap. Sometimes I preach a sermon that I think was mediocre at best and I am pretty disappointed with myself. But someone comes along and tells me that they really appreciated my words or that they "needed" them or were "inspired" by them. They might say, "I thought you wrote that sermon just for me." In fact I had not thought of them at all. But life was thinking about them.

Life is the power lying underneath the skin of our existence, working her will through birthing and dying. Life is the Spirit that massages matter with grace and purpose. Some call this power God.

I hope you are warm and well this week and that life is a culprit deep within your bones.

I am your chaplain,

Gary

The Chaplain's Chart – for the Week of February 3, 2014

I had a graveside service planned for 11:00 Saturday morning. I spent the early part of the morning reviewing my memorial message in my head. Our Honda Civic was parked outside and about 10:15 I went out to warm it up and scrape off the ice. I also let the dogs out to take care of their needs. Sitting in the front seat of the car I cranked the engine. At that very second a white Caravan was racing down our country road. Our Scottie-Poo went racing toward the van. I yelled for him to stop but it was too late. The front wheels missed him but the rear wheel caught him.

Charlie squealed and I ran toward him. The driver slowed down and then stopped. She turned her vehicle around and drove to the spot where Charlie was lying in the road. Upset, she asked if there was anything she could do. I told her that it was not her fault as I scooped Charlie up in my arms. He was panting quite heavily but by the time I got to the front steps of the house he was dead. I wrapped him in a large bath towel and laid him on the pool table in the basement. I wanted Mimi and Emily to have a chance to say goodbye before I cremated him. From there I finished getting ready for the memorial service and drove to the cemetery.

My biggest burden was telling Mimi and Emily at the end of the day. They were at WSU where Em was taking a master dance class. I did not want to call Mimi and tell her on the phone. I knew that both of them would be terribly upset. Emily needed to focus on the class and prepare for Sunday's Dance Festival at the College. As soon as they got home our dachshund, Buster, ran out to greet them in the garage. Immediately Mimi asked, "Where's Charlie?" He would normally be in the car before she could get out of it. I said, "Let's go inside and talk." "Oh," she wept, "Is he gone?" Mimi knew.

And yes, Mimi and Emily's reaction was as bad as I thought it would be.

You should know that Mimi picked Charlie up out of the puppy crate at Chisholm Trail Feed Store. He was the runt of the litter and no one showed any interest in buying him. The price had dropped from $250.00 to $100.00. They were begging us to take him and finally offered $75.00.

Charlie had only one speed – *FAST*. He was not afraid of anything and baited the donkeys, who hate dogs, and the goats. I loved to watch him run through wheat fields. Run is not the right word. He was short and only weighed about 20 pounds. Rather, he would spring up and over the wheat: boing, boing, boing.

Like all good dogs Charlie loved affection. He was an attention hog and always jumped up on the bed to lie beside or on top of Mimi. If Emily was having a bad day and moping in her room Charlie would go lie down beside her. My favorite ranch hand is Jayden, a seven year old who visits us at Soggy Bottom from time to time. One day she was stung by a wasp. She was sitting on the back stoop crying. Charlie sat beside her with his head on her lap.

Like all good dogs Charlie was always trying to steal food off the top of the kitchen counter or the dining room table. He loved to get into Emily's dirty clothes and chew up apparel. More than once we had to give Charlie a deep bath after he had an encounter with a skunk or went swimming in the lagoon.

Nineteenth century American humorist, Josh Billings (pen name for Henry Wheeler Shaw) said, "A dog is the only thing on earth that loves you more than he loves himself." You may remember a line of his in Disney's *Lady and the Tramp*, "In the whole history of the world there is but one thing that money cannot buy – the wag of a dog's tail."

A special blessing to all of you who love and grieve your animals; who search for them when they are missing and rejoice when they are found; and vow you will never get another one, at least until you are at the feed store several months later.

Your Chaplain,
Gary

The Chaplain's Chart – for the Week of March 10, 2014

Guilt is one of the most common feelings of the bereaved. People feel guilty about what they could or should have done for their loved one. Families will demand that every possible medical intervention be attempted to save the life of the dying and still feel guilty when the heart stops beating and the last breath is exhaled. They feel guilty about what was said or not said, unresolved conflicts, or the dirty deeds of the past that haunt them. I have heard many say, "Why didn't I see this coming?" People also feel deep remorse because they did not get to say goodbye or, "I love you," one last time. We know that the people who have the most ambivalent or conflicted relationships with the deceased are the ones who are likely to have the greatest difficulty grieving. You can bet that guilt runs deep in their souls

Guilt is the heart's knowledge of human failure. Guilt is the pain that we feel because of what the church calls the "sins of commission and the sins of omission." Our souls sear with the knowledge of the things we have and have not done that have brought pain into the lives of others. Guilt is the knowledge that we are alienated from one another because of the things we have done to each other. There are little sins and big sins and with them come big guilts and little guilts. People used to talk about guilt trips. Wouldn't it be nice if guilt was only a trip? Trips have beginnings and endings. Sometimes guilt never gets off the boat. Several years ago I wrote:

To decades of guilt
I am yet bound.
It breaks into my sleep at night,
Sin's nocturnal fright.
Embrace me, O Lord
To Thy Peace profound.

In the Christian tradition we have entered into the season of Lent. The word, "Lent," is of Teutonic origin, denoting forty days. The Latin word for the same period of time is *Quadragesima*. Why forty days? It reminds us of the forty days of the great flood, the forty years Israel spent trying to find its way to the Promised Land, and the forty days Jesus spent in the wilderness. Lent is meant to be a season of prayer and penitence. It is the time when we bring our sins and guilt into the light of God's truth and love.

I believe that Lent has no real meaning if there is no possibility of forgiveness or "peace profound." It is not enough to feel guilt and repent. We cannot do it if there is no promise of reconciliation, joy, and hope. To put it another way, Lent can only lead us to resurrection.

I met a young teenager who was having great difficulty in school since the divorce of his parents. His grades were falling and he was getting into fights at school. He told me that he had really done some bad things in his life, but the worst thing was not being able to apologize to his grandmother before she died. I said that I often talked to my mother who has been dead for fifteen years. Perhaps he could talk to his grandmother. "No," he said, "God won't let me." I said, "How about this: You write a letter to your grandmother and tell her everything you are sorry about. Send the letter to me and I will make sure it gets through."

Please don't think I am being facetious. We all are pushing ahead of us a wheelbarrow full of guilt. Lent is the season to unload the guilt. Lent is the time for confession and the promise that forgiveness and peace is God's will for us.

May the Peace that passes all common meaning be with you all.

I am ever your chaplain,
Gary

The Chaplain's Chart – for the Week of April 28, 2014

The Department of Pastoral and Spiritual Care is printing a card-sized guide for those who are keeping a death vigil with a loved one. We always wonder what we should do or say when someone is dying. I often have to coach a family to speak to their loved ones and offer suggestions on what they can do. Some of these ideas come from Dr. Monica Murphy-Williams' book, *It's OK to Die.*

Here they are:

Six Things to Say to a Dying Loved One

1. I'M SORRY – for the pain I've caused you (name the specific issues in your relationship).
2. I FORGIVE YOU FOR – fill in your own words. Be specific.
3. THANK YOU – list all of the special gifts your loved one brought to you throughout your relationship.
4. I LOVE YOU – name the many ways love is expressed in your relationship such as smiles, laughs, good food, trust.
5. IT'S OK TO DIE – I know you are tired. You don't have to hang on. When you are ready to die we will be OK.
6. GOODBYE – Goodbye for now. I'll see you on the other side. Go with God.

Six Things to Do When a Loved One is Dying

1. Continue to talk, touch, and pray.
2. Read from favorite scriptures or poetry.
3. Touch gently, hold hands, kiss.
4. Tell family stories about beloved people, or pets, or events.
5. Sing favorite hymns or songs.
6. Trust what your heart directs you to do.

These are things we should be saying and doing throughout our lives. If these are the disciplines in our daily lives they will be that much more powerful and meaningful at the end of life. They are simple things to say and do that can bring much comfort in our relationships. The sad thing is that if we do not say and do them it is likely that we will feel much regret or even guilt as a result.

These guides will be placed in the chapel and at each nurse's station. I will keep copies in my office. Please feel free to offer them to patients' families.

It really is OK to die. My responsibility as a chaplain is not only to bring comfort to those who are dying, but also encourage conversations about the importance of dying and death in the fabric of our being. Sometimes death is the healer. I am an advocate for gracious dying, and for hospice care – and sooner rather than later. I know that as the end draws near medical procedures give way to spirituality and the holy place of relationships. Let us tend to our souls, our kith and kin while God gives us breath.

So while I still have time let me tell you that I love you.

Your Chaplain, *Gary*

The Chaplain's Chart – for the Week of May 12, 2014

People treat prayer as if it is something to do when all else fails. I am the chaplain, so it must be my job to pray, and if I have done my job well it will be efficacious. In the ICU last week I spent some time with a family whose mother had come through the emergency department. EMS did not know how long she had been down before they started CPR. She was not responsive all day and her blood pressure was slowly dropping. Early in the day I asked if she had a church or pastor and was told that she was not really a "church goer." I got the feeling that prayer was not wanted. Later that day more family arrived and the tone of the dialogue shifted. It was clear that these family members were religiously rooted.

"Would you pray for her?" one asked.

"What would you have me pray for?" I inquired.

The son answered, "A complete and full recovery – just like she was before this morning."

We all know that when a person is "down" and CPR is required it is not very likely that they will ever be quite the same, if we are able to revive them at all. So, if you were the chaplain, or they asked you to pray for their mother, what would you say?

I do not believe that prayer is magic, making everything just the same as it was before. I do believe that prayer is the invitation to enter the presence of God. When I say, "Let us pray," it means, "Let us open ourselves to the Sacred One, the Source of Life, the Being who creates, sustains, and redeems us." May God be with us even through the valleys of disease and death.

In this particular circumstance I prayed that this mother be restored to the fullness of her being. May she be whole as God created us all to be even in the midst of trauma, disease, and dying. That is not the same as "turn the clock back to 0600 and let's start this day over."

Yesterday morning I looked at a young woman in my congregation. She has three boys under the age of ten. Her husband has left their home. Positively grief stricken she looked beside herself in sadness. I held Staci and her three boys in my heart in the earnest petition that God be with them, knowing that marital reconciliation is not likely to happen. I sang in my heart one of the earliest prayers of the church:

> Kyrie Eleison
> Christe Eleison
> Kyrie Eleison

The words simply mean, "Lord have mercy, Christ have mercy, Lord have mercy." When the service was over the middle child came up to me. This is not normal for him. Like most kids he was on his way to the cookies. But I had just a moment to hold him and kiss him on the forehead. He did not protest or squirm. He smiled and then made his way to the cookies.

Prayer is divine encounter in any and every circumstance, even when bodies and marriages cannot be resuscitated.

May you bump into all that is holy throughout the week.

Your chaplain,

Gary

The Chaplain's Chart – for the Week of May 19, 2014

I Thessalonians 5:16-18 reads, "Rejoice always, pray without ceasing, give thanks in all circumstances; for this is the will of God in Christ Jesus for you."

Really? Has Paul lost his mind? Rejoicing always and praying without ceasing? We have jobs to do, appointments to keep, and families to tend to. How can anyone possibly do this?

It is impossible if you think that prayer means to stop everything you are doing, rush up to the chapel, get down on your knees, and say holy words. I believe that prayer is the practice of the presence of God. When we say, "Let us pray," it means: let us enter into the Mystery in whom we live, and move, and have our being; let us open our ears, eyes, hearts, and hands to the Grace of life; be awake to the milieu of God always present to us in every person we meet, the food we eat, and angels laughing with the wind in cottonwood trees. Prayer does not mean that we stop life to say something, but rather that we live life as it is sacred. Here are some prayer experiences that I have lived in the last few days.

Sara came to my table in the café. "I have to show you this video that I took of my grandma on Mother's Day." She pulls the phone out of her pocket, scrolls down to the video. Her grandmother is standing there with her walker. The family had given her a horn, like the kind we used to have on our bicycles. It is attached to her walker. And there is grandma walking forward, honking the horn. How is that prayer? It is prayer because I was invited into Sara's life and family. She shared community with me. The video was cute, even funny. The sharing was precious. That is prayer.

I visited a man Saturday in a nursing home in Newton. He is a member of my parish near Hesston. Steve was diagnosed with esophageal cancer about a year ago. Throughout the year he has had other surgeries for his cardiovascular disease and a bout with cellulitis. Steve has been in denial about the gravity of his prognosis until this weekend. He was lying flat on his back when I entered his room. His fingers were grossly extended and he told me that he had no feeling in his hands or feet. He hoped I would pray with him so that he could relax and take a nap. I ignored the request for a moment and asked how he thought things were going for him.

"Not good," Steve said.

"Do you think you might be dying?" I asked Steve.

He started to weep, and said, "Yes." There was a pause. "What will it be like when I die?" he asked. We talked about that for a few minutes.

"Steve," I asked, "Are you afraid that you might die alone?"

"Yes," he sobbed.

"And I am wondering if you might be afraid that if you fall asleep you might not wake up." Steve shook his head affirmatively.

With his permission I brought in his nurse and I shared with her Steve's fears. I asked that she talk with Steve's doctor about prescriptions for anxiety and depression. At church on Sunday we talked about stepping up our visits with Steve.

Steve invited me into the most powerful and frightening human experience, that reality that he is dying. That is prayer. And yes, I held Steve's hand and I said words inviting God's presence into Steve's life, praying that the Holy Spirit would fill his mind with peace.

Sunday morning I was sitting on the bench on our porch, facing the morning prairie. There was a gentle breeze as I began my silent meditation. Baltimore Orioles chattered away as they repaired last year's nest. The Dickcissel is the most populous bird in Kansas and called out to each other from tree to shrub. Red Cardinals pierced the air with their constant songs. The Blue Jays shrieked false alarums, while the Mockingbird made fun of everyone else. In the end it was not much of a silent meditation. But what a wonder-filled prayer it was.

I wonder at each of you, looking beyond uniforms, equipment, and titles, ever vigilant for the Holy One. Do share with me your stories of wonder and creation, joy and sorrow, hope and resurrection.

Your Chaplain,
Gary

The Chaplain's Chart – for the Week of June 2, 2014

Our lives are the net sum of our choices. We are who we are because of the choices that we make every waking moment of our days. We make choices about the actions we take and the attitude with which we take them. Questions of lifestyle, diet and exercise, vocation and vacation are all answered by choices. Every day in this hospital we meet people who make choices about their health and they are often here because their choices were detrimental to their well-being.

This wisdom has been in the world since ancient times. In

his *Meditations,* Marcus Aurelius wrote, "Begin each day by telling yourself: Today I shall be meeting with interference, ingratitude, insolence, disloyalty, ill-will, and selfishness – all of them due to the offenders' ignorance of what is good or evil." In the book of *Deuteronomy* we read, "I call heaven and earth to witness against you today that I have set before you life and death, blessings and curses. Choose life so that you and your descendants may live…"(30:19) A similar notion is found in the apocryphal book of *Sirach,* "He has placed before you fire and water, stretch out your hand for whichever you choose. Before each person are life and death, and whichever one chooses will be given." (15:16-17)

I invite you to hear these words more as statements of fact than judgmental condemnation. It is like the child who did his algebra homework faithfully every night, but he failed the class because he never turned in the work. It was stuffed down in his backpack or locker at school. Or consider the young dancer who every night stretches and strengthens her arms, legs, and back, preparing for the rigors of ballet training. By making this choice she avoids injury, improves her technique, and enhances her opportunities to be called for a part in the next performance.

Wisdom accepts the reality that our lives are the net sum of our choices. Wisdom also accepts the reality that we have to deal with the choices others make. We do not make life choices for good or evil in a vacuum. Choices impact our relationships, our communities, and our world. The planet responds to human choices about carbon emissions, oil spills in the Gulf of Mexico, the destruction of barrier reefs and marshlands, over-tilling of land and the consequence of erosion. This is not a political opinion but a fact of life.

We have to live with our own choices and the choices of others. I think we spend too much time asking people how they feel about something or what their opinion is about the matter. The real question is what are you going to do? In the world of pastoral psychology there is a time for understanding the history of a person's life and the trauma they have endured. But we cannot grow as a human being if we are fixated on the sad stories of childhood or failed relationships. The choice before us today is water or fire, life or death. What choices will you make for your future today? It's OK to know your family's history but it is far more important for you to select a course of action that takes you forward.

And let's be honest. More often than not we know what we have to do. Do we have the resolution to do it? Every time I go to lunch I have to choose to be a compliant diabetic or not. That's pretty hard when the first thing I see in the cafeteria serving line is a piece of blackberry pie. That's OK as long as I remember that I have a choice.

Blessings to you in all of the choices that you will be making for your future today!

Your Chaplain,
Gary

The Chaplain's Chart – for the Week of June 30, 2014

Trappist monk, spiritual director, peace activist, poet, artist, and author, Thomas Merton, wrote, "Happiness is not a matter of intensity but of balance and order and rhythm and harmony."

Most of us can find plenty of intensity in our lives – our work in the hospital, household chores, relationships, and family. Sometimes we seem to only operate out of intensity. When that happens we become fatigued and our bodies rebel with headaches, backaches, and nasty gastrointestinal disorders. The next thing you know you are not sleeping well and everything just gets worse. It is also a fact that work and sleep take up about two-thirds of our day. So what will we do with the other eight hours?

Can you imagine using those eight hours for:

- ➢ Meals and relationships
- ➢ Meditation or prayer
- ➢ Household work
- ➢ Learning
- ➢ Exercise
- ➢ Rest

I know – I know – that does not leave much time for television. But maybe that is a good thing. Maybe television or Facebook are time dragons that never really bring balance, order, rhythm, and harmony into our lives. Perhaps we should ask that question of anything that we do. Will this project keep my life in balance? Does this event create harmony in our household?

Too often we expect to be entertained. Too seldom do we ask if anything that we do brings balance to our lives. It's really a simple question, yet it can profoundly affect the quality of our living.

What does this really mean? I think it means sitting on the front porch with a cup of coffee thumbing through a prayer book or book of poems. Catching the phrases of songbirds. Lying on the trampoline at night watching stars and comets while you hold the hand of someone you love. Long walks or cycling down country lanes. Lingering meals with dear ones, dining on homemade bread and hearty chowders. Spitting watermelon seeds from the porch swing. Skipping rocks across the pond. Weeding the strawberry patch, eating as many as you can. Long conversations with silence.

Without balance our lives become wobbly and we fall down. The intensity kills us. Love yourself, love your work, and love your family with the gifts of balance.

Now if you will excuse me, I need to take a walk.

Your Chaplain,

Gary

The Chaplain's Chart – for the Week of August 25, 2014

One of the things that you may not know about me is that I like to bake bread, especially artisan breads. I bake white and whole wheat, ciabatta, baguette, French, and the oldest bread recipe – *pain a L'ancienne*. The last one is perhaps the most primitive and simple of all bread recipes using only flour, salt, yeast, and water. I usually bake on a "stone" and use a peel to position the bread on the stone and to remove it. Of course, I sometimes use loaf pans. Some recipes call for two days of preparation, rising, and cooking.

My family hovers around the kitchen while the bread is baking and ask too often, "Is it cool enough to cut yet?" And, of course, they slather butter over the warm bread and devour it greedily. Sometimes a half a loaf is consumed in less than an hour.

I like baking because of the wonder of it. I enjoy working the dough to get the right body and texture. I love the aroma of yeast doing its job as the dough rises, is pressed down, and rises again. I love to bake because at the end of the process I can see a tangible reward. I have worked and created and it brings pleasure to my family and friends.

I have taken up a new line of cooking – making homemade preserves. Dillons food store had raspberries on sale over the weekend. I put up 9 pints and I am waiting to see if blueberries come back. I would actually like to make a triple berry preserve of raspberry, blueberry, and blackberry. The challenge of getting the right balance of acidity, pectin, and sugar to get the preserves to set up right requires a great deal of patience. One of the reasons I like to use fresh fruit is because I get to keep the seeds in the preserves. The flavor is heartier too. So many store bought preserves are nothing more than a flavored paste. Restaurant jellies, jams, and preserves are not much more than a smear of artificially flavored and colored gelatin.

What has any of this got to do with spirituality? Baking and eating are essential human functions. It is primal to our survival. Sometimes we get so caught up in very sophisticated and technological endeavors that we lose touch with the organic needs and processes of life. Sometimes we need to step away from the computer screen, the diagnostic imaging machine, and the microscope to put our hands around a ball of dough and remember what is basic to human life. Bread is a major theme of the Jewish and Christian faith traditions. Bread is essential for our physical and spiritual sustenance. I bake bread, in part, as an expression of my spiritual life. Baking bread requires no doctrine or creed. Bread is its own ritual and symbol.

The Jewish prayer for bread is, "Blessed are you, Lord our God, King of the Universe, Who brings forth bread from the earth." A prayer from the Christian Emmaus community reads:

"We pray then, good and gracious God, that we might recognize you in the breaking of bread today. It is the bread of heaven, the bread of the poor, the bread of our lives. May we recognize you every time we join someone on a journey, every time we share a meal, every time we take bread in our hands."

Baking and breaking bread is a sacred and awesome experience, one that can be shared with any human being on the planet. Every time we do that it is an expression of God.

It is my prayer that, like the dough rising on the floured board, your life will expand to feed and nourish all who come your way.

Your Chaplain,
Gary

The Chaplain's Chart – for the Week of September 1, 2014

The story is told of the little girl who was busy wrapping a large box, about the size of a liquor box. The eight year old was using gold wrapping paper. She was almost finished when her father came home from work. He looked at her project and exclaimed, "What are you doing? Don't you realize how expensive gold wrapping paper is? How can you be so wasteful?" He stormed off to his study.

The next morning at breakfast the father was drinking his coffee and reading the newspaper. He was a little embarrassed about his profusion of anger the night before when his daughter approached him. She presented him with the box wrapped in gold paper. "Here, Daddy, this is a gift for you."

The father took the gift and said, "Why thank you sweetheart." Opening the box he could not see anything inside of it. Again he exploded with anger. "What is the meaning of this?" he demanded. "You don't wrap up a box and give it as a present to someone with nothing in it."

Tears started running down the little girl's face. "But Daddy," she cried, "it's a box full of kisses. I spent all day yesterday blowing kisses into that box for you."

You can imagine the man's shame. He apologized profusely and hugged his daughter.

It is said that years later the child was killed in an automobile accident. The father kept the gold box beside his bed for the rest of his life. Every once in a while he would open it and take out a kiss.

Life is constantly presenting us with gifts, even when we do not see them or appreciate all of the love and kindness that went into their wrapping. Not all gifts are wrapped in gold. Some are wrapped in brown butcher's paper. Some gifts are not wrapped at all.

I appreciate all of the gifts that come my way. I am kissed by the high-fives, the hugs, and the exuberant, "Hi, Chaplain!" It is a gift when someone approaches me and says, "Chaplain, did you know I am pregnant?" Or, "Chaplain, would you pray for my kids?" What a gift it is when someone says, "Chaplain, I am really glad you are here."

Yes, it all sounds sentimental, maybe even corny. But I am old enough to know that the best gifts in life are kisses from friends and family, colleagues, horses and dogs. So take a few seconds and imagine that I am sending you a kiss, thanking you for the inspiration you give me, the joy I have just being in your presence. Collect all of the kisses you can, keep them in a gold box and have enough sense to take one out from time to time, especially when the world is hard and bitter.

I hope this message is my kiss to you.

I am the Chaplain who is here for you,

Gary

The Chaplain's Chart – for the Week of September 29, 2014

Have you heard the joke about the man who said to his wife, "I want to know how you control your temper. You never seem to get angry. How do you do that?"

The wife replied, "I scrub the toilet."

"How does that help you control your anger?" asked the husband.

"I use your toothbrush," she said calmly.

I often hear people say that men and women of faith never get angry. Or, they think that having anger is a contradiction of faith or their relationships with other men and women of faith. But that is not true. We need to understand that anger is a neutral value. Anger can be used very creatively or destructively, but in and of itself anger is amoral.

The first thing to know about anger is that it is a physiological phenomenon. In the human brain, just about in the middle, are two almond shaped bundles of nerves called the amygdala. The amygdala is on the lookout for anything or anyone that might threaten us. When they sense danger the amygdala orders the adrenal glands to release chemicals called catecholamines. These include adrenaline, dopamine, and cortisol. The liver is directed to dump more sugar into the blood stream to provide enough energy for fight or flight. In anger the blood vessels enlarge to carry more blood and oxygen to the heart and blood pressure rises as the heart beats faster. The mind becomes incredibly focused to the point that other surrounding people or events are very peripheral. All of this happens before the brain's cerebral cortex has the opportunity to think through the situation and make a reasonable decision. There are times when we have to make a decision in only seconds and it is anybody's guess whether the amygdala or the frontal lobes will have the day. My guess is that many police shootings happen, not because the officer is trigger happy, but because the body senses an action has to happen quicker than the brain can process all the data. It is important to understand that the physiological foundation of anger is meant to keep us alive. It is part of our protective defense system. The physiology of anger is also triggered when we perceive that someone we love, such as a child, is in danger. The "rush" that so much chemistry enters into the blood stream can take hours or days to level off.

Anger is also an emotional response. In this case the anger is generated by feelings that are not really rooted in an immediate physical threat. We become angry when we think that someone has insulted us verbally, is threatening our relationships (such as marriage) or our financial security. Anger, in the psychological sense is often about control and we often imagine that we have to be in control of everything and everybody to protect and nurture our lives and families. Anger is roused when we cannot get what we want. The emotional needs of human beings often trigger the physiological responses I wrote about above. We hear people say, "He really got worked up." This is about the time we slam doors, scream, curse, write nasty messages with lip stick on somebody's windshield, and give them the finger.

On the other hand, anger can give us the energy to rise to someone else's defense, either physically or socially. I know a woman whose son overdosed on heroin and died. Anger is a major component of her grief. She thought she was the only one who knew such tragedy until she met other parents who felt the same way. She took the energy of her anger and started a blog and a support group for family and friends of those who die from drug overdose.

Always the challenge is for us to understand anger and reflect on those things that tend to make us angry. We can learn about the biological and emotional roots of anger and then how to make the energy of anger a tool for better mental health and interpersonal relationships. I believe that anger can be a gift of God and like all of God's gifts we have to learn how to be stewards of it.

Your Chaplain,
Gary

The Chaplain's Chart – for the Week of October 6, 2014

There is a 13th Century Welsh tale told of Llywelyn, prince of North Wales. John II of England gave Llywelyn a great English hound as a gift. The dog was named Gelert. During the birth of his son Llywelyn's wife died. The prince gave the protection of the newborn child to Gelert during those times when the prince was off hunting or on business. One day the prince came home and found the baby's cradle knocked over. The infant's blankets were soaked in blood and the baby was nowhere in sight. Gelert rushed to greet his master, his muzzle and throat saturated with blood. Llywelyn could only conclude that the dog had killed the child. He drew his sword and thrust it between the shoulders of the hound, piercing its heart. The dying dog yelped in pain. Hearing the yelp the prince's child cried out. Llewellyn rushed into the adjoining room. His boy was on the floor. Beside him was the body of a great wolf, slain by his faithful dog, Gelert. His grave can still be found at a place called Beddgelert.

Like so many of us Llywelyn rushed to judgment and killed his loyal dog – or partner, or friend, or child, or even people we have never met. Being judgmental often causes us to lash out to convict and condemn others, inflicting pain and even death. Jesus constantly reminds his followers not to be judgmental of **anyone**, as is found in Matthew, Luke, and John. The Carpenter insists that we will be judged in turn by the same measures we judge others, and insists that God is the only judge and God alone decides the worth, value, faithfulness, and future of every human being.

Now let's be clear. We all can and must make judgments. We all have opinions, have convictions about what is right and wrong, and make the best decisions we can about everything we do in our lives. We will make a judgment about whether to have a second piece of pie, who we will vote for, and how to deal with a child who has been caught cheating on a test at school. Jesus is not saying that we do not, cannot, or should not make judgments.

But making judgments is not the same as being judgmental. When we are judgmental we attack the person, condemn them, ostracize them, embarrass them or attack them publicly and privately. Judgmental people make no secret of their contempt of the people they have judged. They gossip about them, lie about them, or attack them on public media such as Facebook. When we are judgmental we determine that these persons have little or no value and worth in our eyes and in the eyes of God.

Judgmentalism is woven by the threads of ignorance, anger/ fear, and pride. I start with ignorance because a judgmental person assumes that he or she knows the mind and heart of another human being. In fact, we cannot know the full conscience of another man, woman, or child. We cannot know their relationship with God, regardless of whether they go to our church, mosque, synagogue, or have no religious affiliation. Only God can know the depth of faith and moral agency of any other person. When we think that we know such things we are assuming the mind of God, and such pride condemns us all. In my experience people who are the most judgmental are people who are very angry and or burdened with guilt.

Don't forget that when Jesus is talking about such things he is addressing a community. In his case, the community of disciples, fellow Jews, and antagonists. He thus speaks of judgmentalism as a community sin, one that destroys the families and institutions that are meant to protect and nurture us all. One of the most destructive sins in local churches is that of judgmentalism.

Jesus teaches us that humility and forgiveness are the most important arrows in the quiver of faith. If you find a judgmental arrow in your quiver, break it and burn it, for in the end it will only slay your relationships with others and with God.

I am here to serve you.

Your Chaplain,

Gary

The Chaplain's Chart – for the Week of October 20, 2014

Years ago the chaplain of the Notre Dame football team was a beloved old Irish priest. At confession one day, a football player told the priest that he had acted in an unsportsmanlike manner at a recent football game. "I lost my temper and said some bad words to my opponents."

"Ahhh, that's a terrible thing for a Notre Dame lad to be doin'," said the priest. He took a piece of chalk and drew a mark across the sleeve of his coat.

"That's not all, Father. I got mad and punched one of my opponents."

"The Saints preserve us!" the priest said, making another chalk mark.

"There's more, Father. As I got out of the pileup, I kicked two of the other team's players in the groin."

"Mary, Joseph, and Jesus," the priest wailed, making two

98

more chalk marks on his sleeve. "Who in the world were we playin' when you did these awful things?"

"Southern Methodist," replied the player.

"Ah, well," said the priest, wiping off his sleeves, "boys will be boys."

This week is Pastoral Care week, celebrating women and men who are called to chaplaincy. Chaplains are found in hospitals, the military, industries, prisons, universities and many other places. Just about every religion you can think of has chaplains in all of these places, including Jews, Muslims, Christians, Buddhists, and many more.

People think that a chaplain's job is to make people feel better or to cheer them up. That is possible some of the time. But more often than not comfort does not mean a happy ending. Pastoral care is more likely to mean helping people cling to hope, confirm the value and meaning of their lives, and bring their lives to a close with as much dignity as possible. Pastoral care is encouraging people to make healthy choices for their lives, end or begin new relationships, and take responsibility for their future.

A chaplain is likely to hear confession and grant absolution, baptize a stillborn, offer Holy Communion, officiate at a wedding, and anoint a dying one. Chaplaincy is the work of helping people make end of life decisions such as a durable power of attorney for healthcare or coaching a family toward hospice care.

The needs of hospital staff are never far from my mind as chaplain. And while it seems that I do very little in the midst of a "code blue," I am there to encourage staff, assure them of their competencies, and absorb some of the tension and anxiety that is a part of every trauma. While I sometimes go home at the end of a day thinking and praying about a patient, I always go home thinking and praying for you.

Being a chaplain means that I am here for you.

Gary

Jesus told a parable about the Pharisee and the tax collector (Luke 18:9-14). Both men are in the temple. The Pharisee makes a very public display of his faith and his prayer is this: "God, I thank you that I am not like other people: thieves, rogues, adulterers, or even like this tax collector. I fast twice a week; I give a tenth of all my income."

The tax collector, considered a social pariah in Jesus' day, hides in the shadows of the temple. He will not even lift his eyes toward the altar. His prayer is quite simply, "God be merciful to me a sinner." With the burdens of his life, and fully conscious of his character flaws, he knows he has nothing to brag about. And yet, Jesus states that this man, "went down to his home justified..." Justified here means that he and God are reconciled. He is "saved," meaning that his relationship with the Holy One is restored. He is now "righteous," meaning that he and God are in a right relationship.

I pray with patients many times a day. I hope these are not prayers about me. I hope they are not ostentatious. My hope is that pastoral prayers help patients be reconciled with themselves, their families, and their God. I hope they will find a peace that can only come when we are submissive to God's will for us. Typically my prayer includes something like this: "Give us the courage to do God's will, even when we don't want to, even when we don't like it."

Now it is very important that we understand the difference between what is God's will for us and knowing what might be God's plans for us. George MacDonald wrote, "Doing the will of God leaves me no time for disputing about his plans." In other words the real question about God's will is the kind of person God wants us to be, regardless of the circumstances of our lives, or what stage of the disease process we are in, or our prognosis. God's will for human beings is focused on our love for God and neighbor, our commitment to moral agency, human reconciliation, and God's justice. Thomas Merton wrote, "For each one of us, there is only one thing necessary: to fulfill our own destiny according to God's will, to be what God wants us to be." Doing God's will means being the blessing that God created us to be.

I do not believe that it is God's "plan" that anyone has cancer or any other malady. The challenge of my faith is not whom to blame or ask, "why me?" or "why is God doing this to me?" Doing God's will means that I enter every sorrow or joy with faith that God is with me, no matter what. Doing God's will means receiving both the good and the bad with compassion and hope. Or, as I have often said to my congregation, "God has brought me this far and I can only trust God to take me into God's future."

There is violence, hatred, injury, doubt, despair, darkness, and sadness in the world. The question is not, "whose big idea was this?" or even, "what does it all mean," or "why did it happen?" The question is what kind of man or woman of faith are we in these circumstances. The St. Francis prayer suggests that God calls us to be agents of peace, love, pardon, faith, hope, light, and joy. This is doing God's will. With that said,

May the Peace of God be with you all.

Gary

The Chaplain's Chart – for the Week of November 3, 2014

I wish I could tell you how many church board, committee, and task force meetings I have attended in the past 40 years. I can tell you with all certainty that I will not go to my grave saying, "Man, if I could only go to one more church meeting."

Last Thursday night the most remarkable thing happened. God came to my church's monthly board meeting. I did not recognize him at first. I just thought he was Braden. In fact, I did not know either of them were in the church. Somewhere in the midst of the insurance discussion God was sitting on Staci's lap. Staci keeps the minutes of our meetings and God decided to help and started punching keys. Patiently Staci sent him off on some kind of mission. A little bit later I saw the Holy Prankster on his tip toes prancing into the kitchen with great stealth. A few minutes later he emerged with popcorn wrapped in a napkin like a ball. It had to have been a miracle because there was no sound of corn popping or the smell of hot oil. Again he snuggled up onto Staci's lap. He looked at me from across the table with blue laughing eyes.

Now you need to know that God and I have some history together. For one thing the Creator of the Universe loves eye contact. He gives me better eye contact than any other person I have ever met. In fact, one Sunday he was the only kid in my "Time for All Children" message. We sat side by side on the steps of the chancel and his eyes never left mine. I do not remember what I said but I do remember that this was a holy encounter.

When we found out that Mimi was pregnant with Emily we signed up for the Lamaze class. Never mind that I had graduated cum laude in the previous four classes. It was a requirement of the hospital. One of the techniques was to focus on an image or object during the breathing exercises. The problem was that the delivery room was bare white – walls and ceiling. Mimi decided to focus on my eyes. And guess what I learned looking back at her? God's eyes are brown. We still do that in times of pain or deep decision making.

Some people believe that the eyes are the windows of the soul. Perhaps, but I agree more with Ralph Waldo Emerson who wrote, "The eyes of men converse as much as their tongues, with the advantage that the ocular dialect needs no dictionary, but is understood all the world over." It is with the eyes that I know whether or not I have connected with another human being, despite all the words that are uttered. A patient may tell me that he or she is just fine, but the eyes reveal fear or doubt or anger. I have known patients in deep pain but their eyes were clear pools of hope and confidence. I have known eyes that sparkle, weep, avert, affirm, hide, and blaze with fire. They all tell me something that words cannot express. As Jesus said, "The eye is the lamp of the body…" (Matthew 6:22)

So here's looking at you! And may your whole body be full of light!

I am the Chaplain that is here for you,
Gary

102

On Wednesday morning my wife called me on her way to work. Mimi reported that all of the dashboard lights were on and the warm air from the heater was now cold. She went to the auto repair shop that we use. I picked her up and took her to South Breeze Elementary School where she works. Later that day the mechanic called her to report that she needed a new water pump and thermostat. Since they were going to tear into so much of the engine they should probably replace the timing belt, and oh, by the way, she needs a new tie rod. We picked the car up Friday evening for about $900.00. And the icing on the cake is she also needs a new vacuum hose, another $120.00.

On Saturday morning I put a load of laundry in the dryer and a fresh one in the washer. When the timer went off I hobbled downstairs to put the dry clothes into the laundry basket. The problem was that they were not dry at all. So we went to Sears to find out that they would charge us $168.00 just to make a repair trip, plus costs of parts and labor. The dryer was pretty old and they had a $600.00 model on sale for about $350.00. The clerk told us if we waited until Sunday we could get another 15% off. That, of course, is what we did. Sunday morning that same clerk was not in the store and a different clerk said we could only get 5% off. Mimi looked over the rim of her reading glasses with her fierce brown Italian eyes and said, "We were told 15% and that is what we expect to have to pay." She won.

Do you ever wonder that you accomplish anything at all, given the unexpected and expensive interruptions in your life? I have read somewhere that the average worker has 50 interruptions in the course of a day. If you observe the Emergency Department, it seems to me that it is a long string of disruptions, each trauma or illness getting in the way of treating another.

C. S. Lewis wrote, "The great thing, if one can, is to stop regarding all the unpleasant things as interruptions of one's "own," or "real" life. The truth is of course that what one calls the interruptions are precisely one's real life – the life God is sending one day by day."

Despite our best laid plans, scheduling apps, alarms, and "to do" lists, life keeps getting in the way. Of course these devices are not reality, just our fantasy of how our day should flow. As Lewis suggests, life is what happens to us, and it is the day that God has given us. The question is not how we can get rid of all of those blasted disconnections. The challenge is to fit these interludes into the greater flow of grace. The end of the day is not ultimately measured by what we have accomplished but how we greeted each of these intermissions with patience, kindness, and compassion. Sometimes these disconnections point us to deeper issues that supersede a scheduled deadline.

Keep this in mind when a patient pushes the call light, or a "code" is called during your luncheon, or a doctor or supervisor tells you to drop everything and be of assistance.

And one last thing, you are not an interruption in my work as chaplain. DO NOT apologize for taking my time with you. DO NOT presume I have more important work to do besides you. I am here for you. You are my work. You are such a profound part of my life.

Deep peace of the running waves to you all.

Gary

The Chaplain's Chart – for the Week of November 17, 2014

Throughout any given day in the hospital I may pray with a patient, their family, or a member of staff a dozen times. What is it that people want me to pray for? Good health of course, remission from a disease, the successful outcome of surgery, and peace at the time of death. People also want prayer for love and harmony in their families, reconciliation with loved ones, and courage during times of alienation. Most people want God to bless their work, career, and financial security with providential grace. Once in a while people offer prayers of thanksgiving. Even people who do not typically pray may fall to their knees during a time of crisis when there is real threat to their lives, their families, or their means of living.

There are all kinds of prayer rituals, practices, and formulas. Most of us are familiar with the Lord's Prayer, the Prayer of St.

Francis of Assisi, table blessings such as "God is Great" or "Come Lord Jesus Be Our Guest," and bedtime prayers such as "Now I lay me down to sleep."

As I have grown in faith and practice I have discovered the great power and energy of silent prayer or silent meditation. In part I think this is because I use so many words all day long. I use spoken and written prayers. I am constantly reading, writing, talking, and listening to National Public Radio, or the needs and wants of the people around me. And then there is that constant conversation that goes on in my head. Who are all of those people in there? There are times when I just want all the noise and jabber to shut up, be quiet, and be still.

Going deeper, I want more than anything to be in touch with the real Source of Life. I want to discover the Essence of Being and be in communion with the Unity of Life in whom we all live and move and have our being. You see I am not using the word "God," not because that is not what I mean but because I do not want to jump to conclusions or rush to theology and the truck load of ideas, words, and debates that it brings with it. My hope is to reach beyond all dogmas, creeds, and articles of religion and be at one with the Mother of Ten Thousand Things, to use a Taoist phrase. I want to get out of my head and find my right mind in the Suchness of things. (I know, some of you might already think I am out of my mind.) That means entering into the Divine Reality where there are no false distinctions, no judgments, no presumptions but only the River of Life. That also means I must abandon all of my assumptions about good and bad, birth and death, sacred and profane, or blessed and damned.

How is this possible? It is possible by the constant discipline of silent sitting, mindfulness meditation, or to use a Buddhist word, zazen. The practice finds a quiet place to sit erectly, breathing through the diaphragm, and then the gentle work of patiently quieting the mind. There are hundreds of websites and books on this subject. My favorite is Robert Aiken's book *Taking the Path of Zen*. It is an older book but the meditation instruction is one of the best. I try to spend at least 30 minutes a day in silent meditation.

Now, don't go crazy on me at this point. The discipline of

mindfulness training does not mean that you have to give up your religious faith – Protestant, Catholic, Jewish, or Muslim. There are practitioners of silent meditation in many religious communities. We are not talking about religion here. We are talking about a spiritual discipline. Yes, I still offer the prayers of the church, read scripture, keep a journal, anoint with oil, and bless the living and dying. But my spiritual health requires that I go back to the Deep Well of Emptiness before I can ever know the Word beyond all words. I must sit down, shut up and pay attention. Such discipline strengthens me to be present with all suffering, to enter into the shadows with calmness, and see the Holy One in every human circumstance. It helps me see you and love you just as you are.

Your Chaplain,

Gary

The Chaplain's Chart – for the Week of November 24, 2014

When you read the first creation story in the book of Genesis (chapter one), the constant refrain for each movement of the story is, "And God saw that it was good." At the conclusion of the sixth day we read, "And God saw everything that he had made and behold, it was very good." Paul declared in I Timothy 4:4-5, "For everything created by God is good, and nothing is to be rejected if it is received with thanksgiving, for it is made holy by the word of God and prayer."

Did you hear that? Everything created by God is good. During this season of Thanksgiving the invitation is to look around and see the creation and give thanks. That means paying attention to all of the everyday and very ordinary things and people and remember that they reveal the Creator's hand. I am thinking about the Red Tailed Hawk, the fiery sky of a Kansas sunset, and the swell and heave of the ocean's wave. See that it is good and give thanks.

My top ranch hand is eight-year-old Jayden. She was at the house last night and wanted to help me feed the animals. She was wearing a red satin dress with a bow on the front and moccasins for shoes. Mimi gave Jayden a pair of her socks and found Emily's old muckers. Jayden did not flinch at the cold wind or the stinging rain.

She trooped out to the barn and measured out the goat and horse feed. When we were finished she asked, "Is there anything else I can do?" I love this little girl and give thanks to God that her family is part of our family.

On Friday afternoon I was getting ready to leave my office when I was paged to the Emergency Department. A four-year-old little girl was seizing. I think she had three or four seizures in the ED before we were able to transport her to Wesley Hospital. She required intubation, bagging, and a propofol drip. Dr. De Leon and Dr. Faudere, nurses, respiratory therapists, lab technicians, and diagnostic imaging were in and out of her room. As you know, in an emergency like that, when a child is desperately clinging to life, when the outcome is doubtful, especially when no one knows what is causing the seizures, tensions are extremely high. There are few requests and many demands. No one can move fast enough. The EMS was down a technician and needed someone to go with them. We all looked around and Dr. Faudere said without flinching, "I'll go. Let's get moving."

I do not know how the child faired. But when I left the hospital that night I looked into the night sky and prayed, "Thank you for the privilege of working with these men and women. They are a living expression of all that You have made. They are amazing grace."

You are always in my thoughts and prayers and I hope that your Thanksgiving Day will be a blessed one.

Your chaplain,
Gary

The Chaplain's Chart – for the Week of December 1, 2014

In the Christian tradition the season of Advent is upon us. It is the season of waiting and expectation that God will break into the world through the nativity of the Christ child, Jesus. Jesus is Emmanuel, meaning "God with us." My favorite Advent hymn is, "O Come, O Come Emmanuel, and ransom captive Israel." Yesterday was the first Sunday in Advent and we lit the purple candle in the Advent wreath, the candle of hope. Dare we hope that

God will be with us?

That is an important question in a nation that is struggling once again with questions of race equality. Since the grand jury declined to indict police officer Darren Wilson in the death of Michael Brown we have witnessed protests from Ferguson, MO to Portland, OR. Some were violent with injuries, property destruction, and arrests. Is there hope in the midst of such anger and fear? And what does God's hope look like?

Hope looks like a 12-year-old boy in Portland, named Devonte Hart. Devonte was at a protest rally in the city with his family. He had a large sign that read, "Free Hugs." Sergeant Bret Barnum motioned for the child to come over to him. The boy complied. Sgt. Barnum asked Devonte, "Can I get one of those hugs?" You can see online a wonderful photograph of this large, white, police officer hugging this African-American child. Tears are streaming down Devonte's face. I put that picture on our Church's Christmas tree as an ornament in the hanging of the greens.

Hope is a fifth grade boy who marches outside with his class during a school's fire drill. He sees a group of kindergarten kids assembled next to his class. A five-year-old little girl with Down Syndrome is crying. She is very frightened. The fifth grade boy walks over to her, stands beside her, and holds her hand.

Hope is a high school senior, the captain of the cheerleading squad. She comes across a group of middle school kids who have told an elementary child that there is gold in the middle of a mud puddle. The child walks into the puddle, mud oozing into her shoes. She gets down on her knees, clawing through the muck trying to find the gold. The middle school kids are pointing their fingers at her, laughing and making fun of her. The cheerleader captain walks over to the mud puddle, gets down on her hands and knees and helps the child try to find the gold.

God with us means that we enter into the suffering and fear of others. We may not be able to end racial violence, cure Down Syndrome, or find gold in a mud puddle. But we can be companions of those who are broken, or wounded, or afraid. We can hold hands with those who are dying, sit with the lonely, and honor those who are fighting tooth and nail just to stay alive. The truth is that in the end medicine reaches its limits and human lives are given over to Emmanuel, God with us.

Emmanuel has hands, eyes, ears, and mouths. They are yours. And may God be with you all in this season of expectation.

Your Chaplain,

Gary

The Chaplain's Chart – for the Week of December 8, 2014

I once visited a little girl on a Monday morning who had pneumonia. It was serious enough to require hospitalization but there was no thought that her life was in real jeopardy. Her mother was in the room with her, along with an older sibling and an infant sister. In the course of my conversation with the mother I learned that they had just buried a child on Saturday morning. Like a lot of mothers raising four children the mom looked harried and tired. Yet her strength was palpable as she tended her ill child and the two other children. I was inspired by her calm determination. I asked her, "What is the strength that you draw from that helps you get through this grief and the needs of these children?"

"It is not a matter of inspiration," she said. "I don't really have a choice. I have to care for these kids."

I started thinking about disenfranchised grief and delayed grief. I wondered when she would possibly find the time to process the death of a child and what would be the consequences if she did not. But the mother is also right. She does not have a choice and she must care for the living. Sometimes the clinical needs to be set aside and encourage the practical realities of life.

I have a dear friend who is going through a really rough time in her life. The future is very uncertain, she is not sure what to expect, and solutions are not yet discernable. After commiserating about all of this for quite some time she looked up at me, smiled, threw her hands up in the air and said, "And then there is life."

"And then there is life." There are other children to care for, responsibilities at work, and cows to be milked; not to mention the fact that someone has to do the laundry. And then there is life after the last family Christmas dinner, New Year's Eve party, cruise and vacation. And then there is life after the infant Christening, memorial service, graduation, wedding, retirement, and first job interview.

Life is an inexorable and dynamic process that is not mindful of the joys and sorrows, ecstasies and defeats of human hopes and fears. Unless we completely destroy this planet the sun will rise on the morrow and someone needs to unload and reload the dishwasher.

And then there is life reminds me of the little resurrections that are just as ordinary as every example I have mentioned above. I do not believe that "the general resurrection" is a far off event at the end of time. There are gentle resurrections every morning when you wake up and get out of bed and tend to the responsibilities of your life.

I think of all of the trauma that occurs in our Emergency Department. Some patients are dead on arrival, some are transported to a hospital in Wichita, some are sent to a medical-surgical unit, some die, and some go home. When the patient has left the ED and someone is cleaning soiled linens and disinfecting the bed and equipment we hear over the public address system, "Triage, triage." Or an ambulance backs up to the loading dock of emergency services. "Triage, triage," is Gabriel's trumpet announcing the resurrection and then life goes on.

Pay attention to the reality that life goes on, that God graces us with little resurrections every day. And never doubt that yours too are the hands that restore life.

Your Chaplain, *Gary*

The Chaplain's Chart – for the Week of December 15, 2014

This is the season of angels: plastic angels, styrofoam angels, wooden angels, and porcelain angels. There are angels at the nativity scenes of homes, churches, and in the children's annual Christmas pageant. Angels can be found in jewelry, on Christmas trees, adorning Christmas cards, on the front lawn and the roof of the house. Angels are tattooed on shoulders, forearms, backs, knuckles, chests, and other places on the human body that are best clothed. You can find the word angel on the bib of a baby and painted in red glitter on the butt of a teenager's jeans.

Despite all of this nonsense I still believe in angels, the real kind. Jacob, in the book of Genesis, has a dream of angels going up and down the stairs between heaven and earth. They are carrying messages of the sacred to the profane and *vice versa*. The Hebrew word for angel is *Malakh*, and it means "messenger." There is also the *Malak penov,* meaning, "angel of the presence." Isaiah wrote, "In all their affliction he was afflicted, and the angel of his presence saved them: in his love and in his pity he redeemed them; and he bore them and carried them all the days of old." (Isaiah 63:9)

I believe that there are messengers of the Holy One present to people, bearing their afflictions, saving and redeeming them. There are angels of the presence who carry people when they can no longer walk, shouldering their despair, wiping their tears, and laying their bodies gently into the earth when their last breath has been freed from their mortal bodies.

The work of angels is not some sentiment about mythical beings floating through our imaginations. The work of angels is the work of feeding people, clothing and housing them, healing them, and listening to the stories of broken hearts and wonderful dreams. Angels change the diapers of the young and the old. Angels cook food and serve it. Angels clean bodies when they have had a glorious day in the mud, before surgery, and after every effort at resuscitation has failed. Angels mop floors and take out the trash. Angels work the budget for the millionth time to keep the house or institution alive for another week. Angels write prescriptions, protocols, orders, medical records, notes to the teacher, birthday cards and letters of sympathy.

At the end of the day, when the living room is a mound of boxes and shredded wrapping paper, angels wonder if everybody got what they wanted. Angels survey the sink and countertop piled high with dirty dishes, gravy dripping off a platter onto the kitchen floor, and the dogs nosing the trash can. Angels try to decide whether to clean tonight or in the morning. And these same angels wonder where the family will have their next holiday dinner.

I believe in these angels because I live and work with them every day. Yes, I know they are flawed. Some struggle with mental health or family issues. Some do not go to church even at Christmas and Easter, and might even be repulsed by the idea that I would think of them as angels. Some may not even believe in God, or are very skeptical of the possibility. But at the page of a medical code, or the words "triage," they are back in the angel business, carrying the burdens of the people. If I pay close attention I am aware of a Holy Presence they deliver.

You are one of these angels. Thank you for carrying me with you. May you and all whom you love be whole and blessed during this season of Hanukkah, Christmas, and Kwanza.

Your Chaplain, *Gary*

The Chaplain's Chart – for the Week of December 29, 2014

Our wedding trip to Los Angeles was a wonderful and joyous occasion. Most of the family crazies stayed home and we had a great time making covenants, laughing and dancing. Jeremy and Rachel were resplendent in their love for one another. We got home about 1:00 AM on Wednesday morning, and that evening celebrated the Christmas Eve service at my church in Hesston. We returned home to exchange presents, and on Christmas morning enjoyed a family tradition of pecan waffles. Friday evening I had a wedding rehearsal in Benton, with the wedding on Saturday. Sunday was a day of worship and preparing horse troughs for the next cold blast.

I must confess that I stewed about the Benton wedding. Bride and groom are about 18. She is three months pregnant and has a history of depression, with several hospitalizations in her young life. I worry about post-partum depression. The practical side of me thought of all the reasons why I should have declined to preside at this wedding. But the grace side of me said that it is not my place to withhold the blessing of God. I cannot do that anyway. In truth they could have found a justice of the peace to perform the wedding. That would make their relationship "legal." But there would be no one to pray for their love or offer blessings for their future. I can never fully know the soul of another human being and I cannot know the inner strengths of God's presence already within them.

It is a real challenge to resist the urge to judge and condemn or make assumptions about people. It is a greater challenge to invite everyone to the table of grace, offering them bread for the journey and the cup of restoration and renewal. Such love finds room at the table for those who show up unannounced, those who come in late, and those who complain that they would have rather had white bread instead of whole wheat. There is even room at the table for a couple of kids who, perhaps, could have made better decisions about family planning.

I am not a believer in New Year's resolutions. They are seldom thought out in terms of what we will have to do to meet them. Diet and exercise come to mind. The resolution to be graceful is not an annual event for me but a daily one. The Sacred One must constantly knead my soul for the rising of hope. I hope that your New Year will be one of great gratitude and peace of heart. I close with this Celtic blessing:

> May the new year bring
> The warmth of home and hearth to you,
> The cheer and goodwill of friends to you,
> The hope of a childlike heart to you,
> The joy of a thousand angels to you,
> The love of the Son and God's peace to you.

I am glad to be home with you.
Your Chaplain, *Gary*

The Chaplain's Chart – for the Week of January 5, 2015

Today is twelfth night, the last day of Christmastide. All of our gifts have been put away but our Christmas tree is still up. I plugged it in the other day. It is getting dry but I like the lights. I suppose it will come down sometime this month. No more days off for holidays. In fact, Emily started school today. Normal has returned in the midst of a deep freeze.

For all of the money we spent, the food we ate, the carols we sang, the resolutions we promised, and the miles we traveled, what difference did it make? Have we been transformed and renewed? Have burdens been lifted and hope revived?

I think it makes no difference at all if we think of Christmas

113

as magic. Somehow people imagine that if we just put more lights on the tree or sing "Joy to the World" just a little louder all will be right with the world. Peace on earth will reign down upon all of God's people, relationships will be restored, and daddy won't get drunk on Christmas Day.

But what if the Christmas story is an ordinary event of a young Jewish couple having a baby, just like parents all over the world who are having babies this very day? What if the Christmas story is the common hope of every mother that her child promises a new future? What if the reality of Christmas is that God is manifest every day, disclosing a community of self-sacrifice and radical hospitality to every person? What if Emmanuel, "God with Us," means right here, right now, right in front of us? What if the Christmas promise is now our responsibility to deliver?

Christmastide is the recognition that God uses common and ordinary people for uncommon and extraordinary blessings. Just don't let the holy days fool you into thinking this only happens occasionally to very special people in faraway lands. I have decided that sacred events like Christmas are not offered to make me comfortable. In fact, I do not think that God comforts me to make me comfortable. God comforts me to make me a comforter of other people. And trust me when I tell you that I am a very common, ordinary man.

Think about this poem by A. E. Hamilton:

> Ask God to give thee skill
> In comfort's art,
> That thou may'st consecrated be
> And set apart
> Unto a life of sympathy,
> For heavy is the weight of ill
> In every heart;
> And comforters are needed much
> Of Christlike touch.

I thank you for all the comfort you are to me, and pray that I may bring you comfort still.

Your Chaplain,

Gary

I got home last Thursday evening to discover that the power cord to the heaters in the horses' water troughs had shorted out. The ice was five inches thick. I went into town to get a new power cord, broke up the ice, refilled the tanks, and plugged in the heaters. One down and two to go.

On my way to work on Friday, Mimi called to report another challenge. Emily had gone out of the house to go to school. A few minutes later she came back into the house and said, "Mom, I've got a problem."

"What's that?" asked Mimi.

"The front of my car fell off."

Mimi went out to the garage to discover that in backing out, Emily turned too soon and hooked the front bumper onto the frame of the garage door. Off came the bumper, the fender got scrunched, and the headlight popped out.

I was almost in El Dorado when Mimi called to report the situation. Sitting on the corner of Central and Village waiting for the light to change I heard this terrible squealing and smelled smoke as it plumed out from under the hood. John Fisher GMC was catty-corner from me, not even a half a block away, but I had to call a towing company to haul my sorry SUV to the service bay. Fortunately, Diane Heilman was on her way to the hospital and picked me up. She brought me back in the evening to retrieve my vehicle.

It was a $1,600 weekend.

All that money with so little fun, except for the fact that I will never forget Emily's line, "The front of my car fell off." It makes me laugh. It will go into the family's storybook. And when I think about it, many of those stories are funny.

When my son went to Afghanistan I started a notebook called, "Chris' Great Adventure." In it are all of the photographs he sent home. Copies of all of the letters I wrote to him and all that he sent to me are arranged in chronological order. When he got home from the war I offered it to him. He told me to keep it because he was not ready to have it. Throughout the years he has told me many stories but he is still not ready to have it because he is still editing in his mind all that he saw and experienced.

I would wager that each of us goes home from the hospital with stories to tell, at least once a week. Some are hilarious and some are deeply tragic. We will use these stories to learn from what we have experienced, affirm the value of our work, and create anew our love and respect for one another. We will tell these stories to find some perspective on that which is evil and horribly broken in human beings. I hope we will also find in those stories wonder and awe in all that God has created.

Stories allow us to wrap some boundaries on all that happens to us. A story objectifies all that we have gone through and puts it into perspective. As narrator we can look at life and discern not only characters, plot, theme, and point of view, but also value, meaning, and purpose. In the retelling we might also add a new emphasis or introduce another character into the plot, one that we had left out before. With such edits our understanding may shift and we gain a deeper wisdom.

What is the Bible but a telling of stories both human and divine? It is the story of faith communities and their efforts to align their narrative with sacred imperatives. Never does it come out neat and clean and perfectly synchronized. So we keep telling the stories of battles with the Philistines and the Taliban; babies in our Family Birth Center removed from their mothers by state authority and little Moses set adrift on the River Nile to save his life; burned up serpentine belts and wrenched bumpers and the challenge to be joyful, patient, kind, love one another, and laugh a lot. OK, maybe laugh a lot is not in Galatians but I don't think Paul would mind.

I would love to hear your story. *Chaplain Gary Blaine*

The Chaplain's Chart – for the Week of February 2, 2015

On March 3rd at 6:30 PM, I will be offering the "Living With Loss" support group. If you have known significant loss such as the death of a loved one, divorce, decline of health, or any other important relationship please consider participating. We look at the processes and tasks of grieving. Members of the group will share their experiences and insights. They will give us all gifts for coping and redefining ourselves after loss. I learn from these groups every time I facilitate one. The group session lasts no more than one and a half hours. We meet in the Bluestem Room. There is no fee for the group, no records kept, and absolute confidentiality.

It is amazing the losses we all experience, even decades after the fact. For example, on Saturday I received an email from a person I had never heard of. Her first email asked if I am the same Gary Blaine that was a camp counselor at the Methodist Youth Camp in Leesburg, Florida, many years ago. I affirmed that I was. She then sent me the message that she is the daughter of Susan Crews and wanted me to know that Susan had died on January 3rd of breast cancer. Kerry wanted to know if I remembered her mom and, if so, could I share some of my memories.

I certainly remember Susan, even though we lost touch with each other after I went off to graduate school, some 40 years ago. Susan was a spirited pianist who worked with me in the afternoons during, "Singaree." Imagine 350 campers in a great hall singing "I love to go a wandering along a mountain pass," or "Who comes up the meadow way," or "We poor unfortunates live in a clime that calls for at least three full suits at a time." Anyway, Susan played with such gusto and we had a very close bond. She always smiled and had a wonderful sense of humor. Susan never walked but ran like a gazelle every place she went. Even at night you could see this figure bounding across the campground and you knew it was her. Susan always brought me great joy and it was a delight to be around her.

Kerry wrote that her mother became a music teacher and taught private lessons out of her home. Kerry said that Susan even played the piano in the hospital a few days before she died.

For reasons I do not completely understand I am deeply affected by Susan's death. I can only conclude that I loved her more than I knew. I am old enough now to understand that once in a while God sends us music fairies like Susan to throw a little stardust of song and joy. It makes me think of my daughter, Emily, who is my ballerina fairy, dancing in and out of my heart every day.

May the good Lord bless you with gracious fairies. And don't ever forget that I am the chaplain that is here for you.

Gary

My daughter's doctors are trying to identify the reason she keeps breaking out on the back of her arms, under her eyes, and behind her knees. She seems to think it is allergy related and has given Emily prescription strength Benadryl cream, oral allergy meds, and fluticasone. The other night she was using the fluticasone for the first time. She could hardly bring herself to pump the spray into her nostrils. Shivering she would giggle and say, "I'm afraid." "What if I get it in my eyes?" "Does it smell bad?"

Now this is the same kid who can dance on stage before a couple of thousand people. She might slip or bobble, and maybe even fall. But if she has any fear you would never know it. Emily will work the routine as it is choreographed despite a mistake. And when it is all over you will not see her rushing to the wings sobbing with her face in her hands. Her friends and teachers will say things like, "Great recovery," or "Way to dance through it."

The other day I was working with a patient in the emergency department. His home is in Houston. He is a diabetic and had left his diabetes medications in Texas. On top of that he has a great deal of anxiety. We talked for quite a while and he asked me, "Do you try to follow Jesus?"

I replied, "I try to follow Jesus to the best of my ability but I am still a man."

"You are still a man," he repeated. "And you do the best you can."

"I do the best I can and leave the rest to God," I added. "That is all that any of us can do."

He then asked, "Do you ever have to take a leap of faith?"

I answered, "I take a leap of faith many times every day."

The patient looked startled. "Many times a day?"

"Sure," I said. "When I walked into this room I did not know who or what was behind the door. In fact, I once came into this very room to be met by an individual who was so out of his mind that we had to forcefully restrain him and give him an injection to relax him. When I walk into any room or meet any person I can only trust that God's grace precedes me. My job is to meet the person, encounter the grace that goes before me, and try to do what God expects of me as a chaplain."

I take comfort in the fact that I do not have to be perfect. I will try to dance through it, especially when I slip or fall. Courage comes not as a gift from the Wizard of OZ, but through many rehearsals, more blunders than we care to admit, and the practice of picking up the choreography where we left it. And here is the most radical possibility of all. We meet God in the stumble, the sprain, and even in the break. The Holy Spirit lurks in the wings encouraging us to get up – 5, 6, 7, 8.

I am here for you, counting out the line, believing that you are great dance partners.

Your Chaplain, *Gary*

The Chaplain's Chart – for the Week of March 23, 2015

On Friday I took down the electric rope that encompasses the acre of native grasses that we planted about five years ago. I then mowed around the perimeter, leaving a swath of about 12 feet. I am doing this in preparation for burning off the pasture. The two main players in my pasture are Big Blue Stem and Little Blue Stem grasses. When they first leaf out in the spring they have a blue cast to them. Their root system will reach out about 18 feet wide and six feet deep which helps make them resistant to drought. They also produce their own nitrogen, which means they do not have to be fertilized, unlike grasses such as fescue. But like all grasses the one thing they have difficulty with is thatch. Thatch is the accumulation of dead and dried grass. It can get so thick that new grass blades cannot emerge and thrive. This calls for a controlled burn. Any minerals in the burned grass and weeds are returned to the soil. The heat of the fire warms the soil and jump starts new growth.

Native grasses remind me of human beings. We have many fine attributes and learn how to adapt to our environment. We can get established and develop ways to thrive and expand our lives. But like grass we often get tangled up in dead issues, dried up relationships, and the brittle weeds of failure. We get so overgrown with the tired old fodder of personal problems there is no room for new growth. We need a good fire to burn off the dried straw of our souls and create space for a green and vital future.

The church used to say that our souls need to be shriven. That was understood to mean confession, repentance, and absolution. But I mean more than the release that comes from the recognition that we have all sinned and fallen short of the glory of God. In fact, I do not believe that God simply forgets and we start all over with a clean slate, at least until the next sin rolls around. I think that guilt and release is deeper than that. I think it means that we not only confess, but also let go of that which degrades and demoralizes us. We say goodbye to the old habits that undermine us and make us smaller than God means for us to be. Sometimes that even means letting go of relationships that are destructive and humiliating. Metaphorically speaking, we have to put a match to the musty silage that is choking the life out of our souls. I even think that if we will not do it, God will send someone else to ignite the flames of change and renewal.

Into every life there will come many opportunities for regeneration. We get to practice death and resurrection more than once before our lives come to a close. And if you have been charred and even scarred, just wait for the spring rains to come. It does not even have to rain very much. Just the smallest bit of moisture on a burned pasture brings out fresh green blades of grass. So too, you can be restored with the smallest drops of encouragement, patient friendships, understanding loved ones, moments of silence, and the grace of God who wants nothing more than for you to be restored to the fullness of health.

To each and every one of you I wish you good burns, spring rains, and new beginnings!

Your Chaplain,

Gary

The Chaplain's Chart – for the Week of April 13, 2015

Henry James wrote in *The Middle Years,* "We work in the dark, we do what we can, we give what we have. Our doubt is our passion, and our passion is our task. The rest is the madness of art."

120

Of course, many people would like to think that we work in the full light of education, reason, and experience. There is certainly a lot of truth in that. But even with the many lumens of medical science and best practices some people are not to be healed and die. We are not always sure why. In the areas of social work and ministry things get even murkier.

Last week I met with a man who is a convicted sex offender. He was found guilty of raping his wife or girlfriend and went to prison. His parents are members of my church. I buried his father a few years ago. His mother is in a group home with severe dementia. "Dick" was a special education student as a child and never graduated from high school. As a convicted felon he has not been able to find employment. Both parents were deeply wounded by this history but always took pity on their son and did everything they could to help him. After his father died his mother bought him a new truck. As you can imagine his sisters have now taken steps to prevent him from accessing her and her money.

Dick and his significant other, Ellen, met me at McDonalds. He is overweight, grizzled, and his teeth are rotting. Ellen is a pleasant woman with a speech impediment, who makes a small amount of money selling some kind of product door to door. She is in the process of getting a divorce from a man who is a noncompliant diabetic who wallows in his own waste because he refuses to get out of bed for toileting purposes. Dick has lost his driver's license because of vision problems and cannot drive his new truck. His sisters have barred him from their mother's house and he claims he cannot get to property that belongs to him. And if all of this is not enough, he lost his food stamps because the government claims that he misreported the amount of income his mother has been giving him. I am not sure about that because all of that business is managed through his mother's bank to which Dick has no access and he does not have the intelligence to know how to manipulate electronic transactions. Dick and Ellen are living in a trailer and have numerous debts, including $160.00 he owes for his glasses. They asked to meet with me because they need money for groceries.

After we discussed all of this it was about 6:00 pm and I asked them if they would like to have dinner. Ellen lowered her eyes and seemed embarrassed. Dick asked her, "Do you want something to eat?" She said she wasn't sure. He asked again and I encouraged them both to let me buy them something from the menu. They settled for cheeseburgers and fries. No kudos for me, dear friends. This was only McDonald's for Christ's sake.

I took this concern to my church council on Sunday morning and they agreed to make $250.00 available for Dick's needs. We will pay off the debt to the optical company directly and give Dick a check for $90.00. It is understood that this is a onetime gift from our Samaritan Fund. I picked up the checks from the treasurer last evening and will make arrangements to have them delivered tonight.

There is much about this entire history that is darkness to me. I am not sure that I know the whole truth, not just from Dick, but from the entire judicial and social service delivery system. I do not know how or why people get themselves into such dire straits. I see little light ahead for them and wonder how they will survive.

But we do what we can and we give what we have. It is the least that we can do for the least of these in a very broken world. Perhaps this is the madness of ministry.

I pray you have a week that brings you much purpose and meaning. I am your Chaplain,
Gary

The Chaplain's Chart – for the Week of May 11, 2015

I keep imagining that I am going to have a weekend where the dominant theme is relaxation and rest. Four weekends ago it was Emily's prom. Three weekends ago it was a huge wedding at my church near Hesston. Two weekends ago it was a visit with my brother and his wife. This past weekend I baked bread, did the laundry, and prepared for Sunday's sermon. Sunday was church and an afternoon spent reading eight research proposals for the Institutional Review Board for Wichita State University. I have been on the IRB since last fall. We review all research proposals that involve human subjects, making certain that ethical safeguards are in place to protect them. I also wrote an essay for the palliative care chaplaincy class I am taking at Cal-State. For Mother's Day

I prepared Mimi's request for chicken with Chinese peanut sauce, dinner for eight. Sunday evening I watched the season finale of *Wolf Hall* on PBS about Thomas Cromwell, under the reign of Henry VIII.

I would love to have a weekend on a trout stream in Montana. No phone. But I have to also confess that despite all of the busyness of my life I am fulfilled. I am engaged in work that I think actually benefits human beings. That is not something I can say about parish ministry in general, though there have been moments. I am blessed with multiple intellectual challenges and so far the mental capacity to engage them. I love ethics, theology, literature, art, pastoral care, and poetry. They are my friends. And I can say that I have never been happier in marriage and family as I am with Mimi and Emily.

Of course many people would have no interest in any of these activities. Most would think them boring. That's all right. The real question is whether or not you are engaged in life. Do you reach out to grab the brass ring, climb the next mountain, run the next marathon, and face new challenges? What engages your mind, imagination, and energy? And most importantly, do you see these activities as drudgery or one more burdensome responsibility? Or is your body, mind, and soul engaged in work and ideas greater than yourself? Are you elevated and inspired?

I recently spent some time with a woman who is afraid of just about everything. Her husband loves sailing but she will not sail with him. She has traveled to many places around the world but none of them are comfortable places for her to be. Her travels are those of an alien. Sonic is the place she would choose to eat because the food of different countries or regions is an adventure she is afraid to taste. She has no work and seldom ventures out of the house except for church, shopping, and family events. She spends most of her time watching television and TV programs are her frame of reference for most of her experiences in life. She does not meet the diagnostic criteria for agoraphobia but is a timid soul. Ralph Waldo Emerson wrote, "Life has a flavor the protected never know." Sadly, my friend knows little of the flavor of life.

So, dear friends, what are your plans for next weekend? If you are not sure come and visit us. We have firewood to cut, barns to shovel, fences to mend, animals to tend, poetry to write, essays to revise, strawberries to harvest, vegetables to plant, and books to read. May God richly bless your mind with wonder and curiosity!

Your Chaplain,

Gary

The Chaplain's Chart – for the Week of May 18, 2015

I asked my congregation on Sunday if they wanted me to keep praying for rain. They answered back with a resounding, "NO!" Even the farmers thought we have had enough, at least for the time being. We have measured 12.75 inches of rain for the month of May, 4.5 inches this past weekend. There are huge sections of wheat fields that have been bowled over by water. Our pasture is slick with mud and animal waste. It's the kind of mud that will suck your boots off. I have said before that is how I will die. The muck will hold my feet in place while my body falls face down in the goo. I will not have the strength to bear up against the suction and stand up straight. My wife and daughter will look out the dining room window and say, "What the heck is he doing now?" An hour later they might think it is time to wander out and see if I am OK.

Speaking of Mimi, she has been fretting over a Piping Plover's nest that is in our driveway. You may know the Plover as the Killdeer. They build their nests in pastures, typically made of stones. It is very difficult to distinguish the pebbles from their eggs. A few days ago there was one egg in the nest but now there are two. Plovers can lay as many as four eggs. Mimi rolled the trailer from the lawn tractor to one end of the driveway and put a chair on the other end to keep people like the mail carrier from running over the nest.

Plovers run around on the ground and lift up a high pitched piping sound or wail. If they think their nest is in danger they will flop around on the ground some distance away from the nest. Their strategy is to make a predator think they are injured and vulnerable and draw the dog, coyote, or cat away from its young.

All day Saturday and Sunday Mimi kept looking out the front window to see if the hen was on the nest, worried that the eggs would be flooded, and kept rearranging the trailer and the chair. She has become like the Plover hen, figuring out strategies to keep the young alive.

Sitting in rounds this morning I thought that we too are like Plover hens. We keep rearranging medications and various therapies to protect and heal the vulnerable. When we have tried every medical protocol available to us, admitting that we don't know what to do with this patient, we still care for them. We practice the healing arts that are known to us. We offer every comfort care measure. We tender every ounce of dignity that we can muster, even to the dying, the noncompliant, or the ornery patient.

Hopefully, I will never see you flopping around the halls or patient rooms warding off evil or death. But you will not abandon the nest until new birth has emerged, the chicks take to flight, or the egg is no longer viable. New nests will be made and fresh eggs will be laid. The work of tending sick ones never ceases, even when the flood waters rise.

Many blessings to all you birds. With much love, I am your Chaplain.

Gary

The Chaplain's Chart – for the Week of May 25, 2015

Several of you have said that we should get a "do over" on this past weekend. Many picnic and camping plans were washed away.

We had several more inches of rain at our place, Soggy Bottom. One of our large mulberry trees split down the middle. One half fell into our corral and the other on the fence to our pasture. It landed on top of a T post, where it still rests. The post was driven straight down into the ground. All of the electric rope is still connected, but the top strand is now at ground level. Of course I could not get my chainsaw to work. It is over ten years old and I will probably need to buy a new one. This will be my summer physical fitness program.

I mentioned to you last week the plover who has built her nest amongst the pebbles in our driveway. She has three eggs now, and she sat on her nest through all of the rain. I went to get the mail on Saturday. She moved off her nest and charged me. Her wings were spread out and her tail feathers were straight up in the air as she squawked at me.

The mud in the pasture is worse than I last wrote about. This afternoon I will have to lug a 50 pound sack of feed out to the horse barn. Even with four-wheel drive I could not motor through it. The horses and donkeys were reluctant to walk through the slurry of mud and waste to the pasture where an abundance of grass awaited them. I had to put a rope on Bama, our alpha horse, to get them out there. He kept murmuring, "You old fool. One of us could slip and get seriously killed."

We know that several people have been killed in Oklahoma and Texas over the past week. Firefighter Jason Farley was swept away in flood waters in Claremore, OK on Saturday night. He was attempting to save another life when the waters of chaos took his own.

Wheat fields are laid down where I live, as much as 90% in some cases. It might be possible to have a "salvage harvest," but it will still represent a significant loss of income.

Despite all of this a farmer told me on Sunday, "My dad always said that we must be thankful for all of the rain we get." Imagine that! Giving thanks in every circumstance that life gives us. I do not mean the prayer of thanks that says, "Thank God we did not have it as bad as people in Austin, Texas." Or the prayer that says, "I thank God I was spared," inferring that God did not spare the life of a next door neighbor whose home was blown away by a tornado.

The Psalmist declared, "I will bless the Lord at all times; his praise shall ever be in my mouth." (34:1) He does not say, "I will bless the Lord when things are going my way. I will bless the Lord the day I win the lottery. I will bless the Lord when I get that promotion." As paradoxical as it seems, perhaps even counterintuitive, gratitude is the life force that carries us forward, regardless of the tragedies and circumstances that surround us. This is the wisdom of the graveside prayer, "The Lord giveth and the Lord taketh away. Blessed is the name of the Lord." Prayers of thanksgiving remind us of the hope and promise that is our life in

126

God. Without gratitude we become embittered by all of the storms of life. Ann Voskamp, author of *One Thousand Gifts,* wrote, "I have lived pain, and my life can tell: I only deepen the wound of the world when I have neglected to give thanks…"

At this moment I give thanks for the gift of life that God has given. You are in that treasure trove of blessing. I am thankful for you. And I hope you remember that I am here for you.

Your Chaplain,
Gary

The Chaplain's Chart – for the Week of July 27, 2015

I have been swimming laps at the YMCA for the last several weeks. The other day at the pool a man was getting out of the middle lane and headed for the men's locker room. I slipped into the lane and started swimming. A few minutes later the man came back and saw that I was in the lane. There was obvious disappointment on his face. A woman was swimming in the outside lane. On the inside lane a young lady was at the shallow end of the lane. She had glasses on, was holding onto the side of the pool and just seemed to be bobbing in the water. Several people were impatiently milling around the end of the pool, obviously waiting for one of us to finish. I know that lanes can be shared, but if you are a drunken swimmer like me, it is a risky venture for others.

I also know that most pools are pretty strict about keeping people out of the lap lanes if they are not swimming laps. So after a few minutes I mentioned to the life guard that the young lady at the shallow end of the inside lane was not swimming laps and perhaps she could be invited to swim in the general swimming area. She said, "No, it's OK." So I went back to my laps. After thirty minutes I got out of the pool and made my way to the hot tub. I confess that is the real reason I swim laps. Several minutes passed and I noticed the door of the family locker room open and a woman emerged with a mechanized wheelchair. She guided the chair over to the pool lift and then went to talk to the young lady at the end of the pool. The young lady paddled over to the lift and strapped herself in. The lift hoisted her out of the pool and she scooted over to the wheelchair.

She then drove herself into the locker room.

I felt about two inches tall. When I got out of the hot tub I went over to the life guard and apologized. She said, "It's OK. Don't worry about it."

What happened here? All I could see of the young lady in the lap lane was from her shoulders to the top of her head. I could not see what was beneath the surface. I could only see what was topside. Based on my shallow observation I made some assumptions about what she was doing and then presumed to inform the life guard how to run her pool.

We all do this, don't we? We only know people superficially. We only know what is apparent and what is visible. It is like thinking you understand humanity because you watch television. We do not know others at any real depth and make assumptions about them and presume to know what is in their best interest. We make judgments about people with the least bit of information. The results are, at the very least, embarrassing for us and the people we imagined we knew and adjudicated corrective actions. We become alienated from one another and from God. It is morally offensive and too often leads to prejudicial assumptions that belittles people or condemns them to our fears and biases. This becomes the seedbed of discrimination, fear, and hatred. That is why Jesus repeatedly tells us to judge no one – no exceptions!

I hope you will join me in looking into the depths.

Your chaplain,

Gary

The Chaplain's Chart – for the Week of January 4, 2016

We returned from our trip to Atlanta, GA late yesterday afternoon. Unbeknownst to us, our niece, Vita, was hospitalized on the Monday we started our journey. Her hemoglobin had dropped significantly, and they still do not know why. She was placed on a BiPap machine because her carbon dioxide levels were too high. She will probably be on Lasix the rest of her life and require oxygen as well. At this time we do not yet know what the central issue is, if and when she can go home. My suspicion is that her Noonan's syndrome has dropped to a new low and will plateau at that level for some time.

Despite all of this Vita is emotionally and spiritually vital. She takes each event and medical response with a great deal of equanimity and calm composure. There is a Zen like quality of receiving, accepting, and letting go. She has dealt with Noonan's all of her life. I have known her since she was three. And never in all of that time have I heard a word of self-pity fall from her lips. Yes, she feels pain, and I am sure that she gets discouraged from time to time. But I have never witnessed a bone shaking dread of her disease or the final outcome.

My last words to Vita were, "I love you, and Godspeed." She lit up, smiled, and said, "Oh, thanks."

I truly marvel at her courage and strength of soul. It is what got her through college with a 3.0 GPA, and her bat mitzvah. The strength of her soul fought cancer and saw her through two open heart surgeries. I love her and I am extraordinarily proud of her. And I can never forget that her name, Vita, means "life."

Vita is both the exception to and a guide for a society that thinks every inconvenience is a personal assault from God almighty; or a difference of political or religious conviction is a cause for rabid offense; or an unconventional lifestyle requires judgment and punishment on our part. Vita loves every member of our whacky family and is genuinely interested in whatever we are doing. Ambrose Redmoon wrote, "Courage is not the absence of fear, but rather the judgment that something else is more important than fear." I think for Vita there are several things that are more important than her disease and its fatal prospects, not the least of these is her family and her Jewish faith.

Speaking of Jews, we read from Joshua 1:9, "Be strong and courageous. Do not be frightened, and do not be dismayed, for the Lord your God is with you wherever you go." Wherever you go includes the Coronary Care Unit, diagnostic imaging, various laboratories and clinics. It can also include schools and universities, homes and farms, churches of every description, track and field. You don't have to live too long before you realize that accidents, diseases, traumas, and even death can be just around the corner. But it is important to remember all of the things that are more important to you than fear.

For me the things that are more important than fear include my life with God, with my family, with my friends, with my work, and with you. I am very pleased to have been returned safely to you.

Gary

The Chaplain's Chart – for the Week of January 11, 2016

It was too cold this weekend for me to do much out of doors, and I resigned myself to indoor tasks. Like most Saturdays I did the laundry. I baked two loaves of whole wheat bread. I watched the Chiefs football game as I worked on cleaning my study. Cleaning my study, two years past due, was an industrial strength project. I also worked on Sunday's sermon, which continued into early Sunday morning. Except for church, my Saturday projects continued into Sunday. It all sounds pretty mundane, doesn't it?

Would you believe me if I told you that the extraordinary finds its way into the ordinary? Or to put it another way, all which is sacred is found in all that is material matter. The holy is at work as dough rises, soap and water baptize dirty clothes, and chaos is restored to order as books are put back on their shelves and papers are filed into folders and cabinets. Bread, water, and order are religious themes that constantly appear on the human agenda.

The Sacred blossoms beyond the immediate experience or activity. My sermon, "How I Read the Bible," seems to have been helpful to some people in my church and in my online reading group. The bread is always well received by family, especially when it is still warm and lathered with butter. We won't have to wear our cleanest dirty shirt this week. And when I finish cleaning my study this evening I can get back to my writing and editing work.

I sent a picture of the bread to Vita, still in the CCU at Emory Hospital. I try to text a photo and message of hope to her every day. She texted back, "The bread looks so homey and warm. When I'm back home you're gonna have to visit again, so we can go out to eat and so I can get some of your cooking. I wish you a good night's sleep."

You see, these very basic and human processes of everyday living bear the seeds of God's love and grace, hope and joy. We often do not think about that as we add the laundry soap and softener to the washing machine, or mix in the molasses to our warm water and yeast to start the fermenting process. This is how I understand the incarnation of God, with us since the big bang 13.8 million years ago, manifest anew in the life of Jesus and all of the great teachers of wisdom, and sneaking out through all of the glory of creation and daily life. I mean all of the glory of creation and daily life like washing the dishes, vacuuming the house, changing the oil, and going to the parent teacher conferences. Of course it also means the beautiful sunset of a Kansas evening, a quiet dinner with friends, or the way my mare, Sapphire, whinnies and runs up to nuzzle me.

Can you imagine the real power of medicine with the understanding that all we do in our hospital is the expression of God's love among our patients and one another? I believe that you – cooks and dishwashers, nurses and technicians, pharmacists and surgeons, housekeepers and mechanics – are the presentation of the One who creates and makes whole. Do you see why I am so inspired to work with you?

Gary

The Chaplain's Chart – for the Week of January 18, 2016

I grew up on the Gulf of Mexico, and spent a lot of time fishing, swimming, and scuba diving in her warm waters. One of the things I liked to do with my friends was seining. A seine net looks something like a tennis net but smaller. The net is of much finer mesh and may be six feet long or more, and about two or three feet high. There are weights on the bottom of the net and poles on each end. The poles are held by two people who walk through the surf, pulling the net between them. Or, the poles are pounded into the sandy bottom. Either way, the seine net would catch whatever filtered through. It was used mainly to catch bait fish, but we would also catch blue crab and an occasional flounder or white fish. Every once in a while we would snag a horseshoe crab whose legs and tail-spine would get snarled up in the net. Inevitably there would be some seaweed and garbage like beer cans or a stray sneaker.

We can think of the human soul as a seine net. The soul catches all kinds of life giving and enriching gifts from the sea of God's grace. I think of Mimi, Emily and all of my children and grandchildren. There are friendships: old, new, and renewed that have journeyed with me for many years. Experiences of birth, disease, old age, trauma, conflict, losses, tribulations, and death have given me little glimpses of the Mystery I call God. These include the vistas of the Great Smoky Mountains, putting my ear on my grandfather's chest to hear his heartbeat as he lay dying, fly-fishing, my mother singing "Somewhere Over the Rainbow" as she was vacuuming the house, hearing the confession of an elderly person for a youthful indiscretion fifty years old, dipping graham crackers into a mug of milk with Emily when she was very young, and being struck by a beautiful turn of phrase in the Psalter. This morning as I was driving to work I watched the sun rise up from the eastern horizon and the hymn popped into my mind, "Christ Whose Glory Fills the Skies." Not a bad catch for a cold Monday morning.

But in all honesty, our souls also net garbage. I think of rotting guilt or shame that weighs us down, not only for the sin that created it but also our inability to know in our hearts that we are forgiven. There is also the refuse of parents or teachers who belittled us, like my father who often told my sister, "You haven't got the sense God promised a Billy-goat." The sad thing is that she grew up and believed it all of her life. She has been emotionally and spiritually crippled for sixty-four years. And there are many spiritually wounded people whose minister or priest degraded them for asking questions, wondering, and doubting. Soul abuse can rip huge tears in the human heart that renders their spiritual net deeply aggrieved.

The good news is that the human soul can be repaired. You have to take it out of the water onto the beach and restitch the web, sometimes reconnecting netting, or restitching the netting to braille lines or anchor lines. I love the image of sunbaked old fishermen sitting on the beach weaving lines of thick manila or nylon twine, sharing huge fish tales, as they mend their nets. Perhaps the church should intentionally have mending sessions in the basement with lots of coffee, sandwiches, and all of the needles and line that every good soul needs to be rewoven. Of course, that means that we have to love the soul enough to mend it.

Much love to you, dear ones.

Gary

The Chaplain's Chart – for the Week of January 25, 2016

Can you imagine trying to read a book or magazine where there is no space between words or sentences or line breaks between paragraphs? You cannot paddle a canoe without ever taking the paddle out of the water. Did you know that one of the reasons why Norwegian school children excel in academic studies is because they are given 75 minutes of recess and playground time a day? One of the ways to teach people how to draw is to focus not on the subject but the space around it.

Likewise, silence is essential to my daily spiritual discipline. Yes, there is the reading of scripture and the prayers of the church. But they are only words in a life that is full of conversations, sentences, sermons, articles, columns, poems, and books. The meaning of the words become lost in the noise they create. There must be silence in my prayer life if even sacred words are to be received.

The events of my ministry, both joyful and sorrowful, need a silent space to be received into my soul where meaning and purpose are created. Let me give you an example. Last week we received into the Emergency Department a patient who had been in an automobile accident. It happened on the day that was so icy. Apparently she went into a slide and T-boned a truck that was parked on the shoulder of the Interstate. The accident happened about 11:30. A man on the scene felt for a pulse, found a weak one, and started CPR. Because the weather and road conditions were so dangerous EMS could not get her into the hospital until 13:30. She was pronounced dead at 13:35.

The woman was only 36 years old. There were no apparent broken bones or any signs of injury except a bruise from her seat belt. With a possibility that her eyes might be harvested, ice packs were to be placed over them. She had contacts and eye drops were administered to aid the removal of them. The drops pooled and then ran down the side of her face, as if she were tearing. I looked into her dead brown eyes and thought how young she was. It was an eerie feeling.

What do we do with experiences like that? We talk about it of course. We might chart about it. In some cases there might be incident reports to write or a debriefing. But when all the words are said or written, where do you take the memory?

I take it to a quiet place such as my office or the chapel. I might sit with it on my front porch in the country. I sit in silence. I release the experience to eternity. In this case I give her up to God. I let her and the memory go. I listen to the airs of grace that take her away. I bless and release her back to light and stardust.

Brother David Steindl-Rast teaches us that silence is the attitude of listening. "Only in silence will we be able to hear that gentle breath of peace, that music to which the spheres dance, that universal harmony to which we, too, hope to dance."

Spiritual discipline for me is resting quietly and silently in the mystery of the divine presence of God. Come and sit with me some time.

Gary

The Chaplain's Chart – for the Week of February 8, 2016

On my way home from work every day I listen to Radio Kansas public radio. The music in the afternoon is typically "classical," but the playlist often includes contemporary music. For example, on Friday I heard the theme song from the film, *The Magnificent Seven.* The music is really quite beautiful, ranging from the triumphant to the subtle. Because I was not watching the action on a screen I was able to listen carefully to the music. Clint Eastwood's composition, "Claudia's Theme," from the movie, *Unforgiven,* is a remarkably sensitive piece that stands in strange contradiction to the violence of the movie. You probably have many movie or TV musical favorites that might range from "Laura's Theme" in *Dr. Zhivago*, to the television Western, *Rawhide.*

When I was serving a church in Toledo, I would often slip into the chambers, the room that houses the pipes of our organ, while the organist practiced. I often thought that when I die I would like my ashes stored there that I might be resurrected with Gladys Rudolph playing Bach's "Toccata and Fugue in D Minor." His "Jesu, Joy of Man's Desiring" continues to inspire me. And what about all of the hymns, both glorious and quiet such as Martin Luther's "A Mighty Fortress is Our God," and "Calm Soul of All Things Make It Mine," based on the poem of Matthew Arnold? Who does not love George Handel's "Hallelujah" chorus or Franz Gruber's "Silent Night, Holy Night," or John Newton's "Amazing Grace?" I have known parishioners who went to church on Sunday mornings not to hear the preacher but to hear the music.

Many years ago, I worked in a psychiatric hospital in Atlanta, GA. One summer we decided to take some patients from our adolescent unit on a camping trip. Many of these patients had "behavioral" issues and abused drugs, mostly marijuana and LSD. We imagined that they would enjoy singing around the campfire. James Taylor and Rod Stewart were very popular with them at the time. Interestingly, no one knew the lyrics to their music. What they knew were old church hymns such as "Rock of Ages" and "I Love to Tell the Story."

Friedrich Nietzsche once said, "Without music, life would be a mistake." Deeper than that, I believe that music resonates with the human soul more than any other human activity. I love literature and poetry, but nothing touches my heart more profoundly than music. In fact, I think there are a lot of church hymns that are butchered by the words. The tune alone is sufficient for inspiration. There is something in the timbre of music that not only distinguishes notes but also resonates with the human soul and the hope for clarity. Or to put it another way, Mozart's "Piano Concerto #20," often helps me make more sense of the world than any newscast, political reporting, or commentary could ever possibly offer.

We know that music can, at least temporarily, improve cognition. I believe that music offers tranquility and inspiration. There is pretty good evidence that music can also foster creativity. I like to listen to Bruce Springsteen's *Wrecking Ball* album when

I am cleaning the kitchen or baking bread. I also like to put on headphones, lie flat on my back, and listen to Enya to relax and meditate. Her song, "Orinoco Flow" always pushes me into the tides of harmony. And there is nothing to lighten your step like an Irish jig.

Music is good for your soul. St. Augustine said, "He who sings prays twice." I invite you to the prayer of music. Take some time to really listen and allow yourself to be caught up in the instrumentation, melody, rhythm, pitch and tone. Allow music to take you out of yourself and into the spheres of creativity and passion. As ever,

I am here for you. *Gary*

The Chaplain's Chart – for the Week of February 29, 2016

Last week I took Friday off for the purpose of rest and writing. Thursday evening I learned of the mass shooting at the Excel Plant in Hesston, KS. I left our house about 8:30 Friday morning, visiting shops and stores in Hesston. I also visited Showalter Villa, just a few blocks from Excel. At 11:00 I met with the Hesston Ministerial Alliance and we began planning the Harvey County Community Service of Sorrow and Hope. Following that meeting I went over to the Villa and conducted two debriefing meetings for their employees. I got home sometime after 5:00. We had a second planning meeting at 8:00 Saturday morning. I spent the rest of the day working on my Sunday service and preparing for my meditation on sorrow for the community service.

Sunday involved services at my church. At 1:30 I attended a Town Hall meeting to discuss Hesston's budding recovery plan. I tried to take a little nap before the service but could not sleep. The Community Service saw somewhere between 1,500 to 2,000 people. It was a blend of messages ranging from sorrow to assurance. There were wonderful pieces of music, including hymns such as "Abide with Me," and "Precious Lord, Take My Hand." The Hesston College Bel Canto Singers offered, "I Will Lift Mine Eyes." Jason Jones offered the solo, "You'll Never Walk Alone."

136

Monday morning I was called by one of the first victims of the shooting rampage who wanted to talk with me. We spent an hour in conversation. The rest of the day I answered emails, but was finally able to take a nap in the afternoon.

I have two thoughts about our journey from grief to recovery. The first is my certainty that this community is very strong and will pull together. The FBI field director put out a call for food and beverage for the nearly 180 agents and officers, and it was provided, almost instantly, by the community. One of the agents said, "We have never seen such a supportive response from a community in a situation like this."

My second thought is that the road to recovery will be jeopardized by the rush to healing. We will want everything back to "normal" instantly. We will not take the time we need to fully explore the depth of our wounds not just physically, but also, mentally and spiritually. It will take time and intentional processes to ferret out the anger, guilt, and fear that will haunt many people for a very long time. There are some Excel workers who will not be able to reenter that building and I worry that they will become ever more isolated.

I am deeply humbled by the opportunity that was afforded me to work with the Hesston Ministerial Alliance. They came together quickly and worked with a deep and profound pastoral sense of the crisis. Their thoughtful compassion embraced not only those who were killed and wounded, but also the family of Cedric Ford, the lone gunman.

If you would like to receive a copy of my meditation just let me know. I can email one to you. I am glad to be back here with all of you. *Gary*

The Chaplain's Chart – for the Week of April 18, 2016

You may recall that between Christmas and New Year's Day, Mimi, Emily, and I went to Atlanta to visit Mimi's niece, Vita, and her mom and dad, Anna and Robert. Vita was in the ICU at Emory University Hospital. She remained there nearly a month after we returned home. At that point Vita was given the option of ventilation

137

and placement in a care facility or going home on hospice care with her BiPap machine. Vita's passion is her family and she chose to go home on hospice care. They thought she might live two weeks. Monday, April 11, Vita celebrated her 29th birthday.

On Wednesday we received news that Vita had a number of pressure sores on her forehead and face from the mask of her BiPap machine. They were very painful. The hospice nurse suggested that they take longer breaks off of BiPap and increase Vita's morphine use to manage both pain and anxiety. Thursday evening we learned that Vita had gone off of BiPap completely. I told Mimi, "It won't be long now."

Vita died at 1:30 Friday morning. The fact that she died is not very remarkable, but how she died is extraordinary. Vita was lucid almost to the very end. She would fall asleep and everyone thought, "Oh, this must be the end." A little while later she would wake up and ask for pen and paper. And do you know what she did? She wrote "Thank You" notes to her family and friends. I understand this went on for hours. Toward the very end Vita was in a deep sleep and her rabbi decided that there was nothing more that he could do and decided to go home. As he got to the door Vita woke up and started waving frantically for the rabbi to return to her bed. She reached up to him and when he bent over she gave him a kiss.

Jewish funerary practices avoid embalming and burial takes place as early as possible, even within twenty-four hours. There is no viewing of the body, which is treated with utmost dignity and respect. Vita's burial was held on Sunday morning.

Anna had asked Vita to send her a sign after her death that she was "safe," if that was at all possible. Anna is an avid bird watcher. After the burial and all of its customary rituals, a hawk circled over the grieving family. It landed on a tree and kept a watchful eye on these loved ones. Then it soared over them one more time. Mimi said that the light so shined on the bird that it seemed to glow like a fire. That was sign enough for Anna.

To her last breath, Vita died as she had lived, with great purpose. Her purpose was family and friends, richly seasoned with courage, joy, love, deep faith, and profound gratitude.

Next Saturday Mimi and I will fly to Atlanta for the

memorial celebration of Vita Leo Brown's life. We will return Monday evening.

It is hard for people to imagine that we can die with meaning and purpose. Vita showed us how to do that. I am deeply humbled by all the lessons she taught me in life and death. Who ever imagined that a frail, tiny person who suffered all of her life with Noonan's syndrome would be such an exquisite teacher? Thank you Vita.

And may God richly bless each and every one of you.

Gary

The Chaplain's Chart – for the Week of May 2, 2016

In the book, *Compassion*, by Nouwen, McNeill, and Morrison we read, "What really counts is that in moments of pain and suffering someone stays with us. More important than any particular action or word of advice is the simple presence of someone who cares." I hope I am that to you. Since I have been here my constant refrain has been, "I am here for you." As I have said on many occasions, pastoral care can be very basic: Show up, shut up, and listen.

People often ask me to give them some words or phrases they could use with a patient or friend who is in distress. Many years ago a neighbor who lived down the street from us called me in utter panic. As soon as I stepped out of the house I saw a fire truck and ambulance at her door. I entered their home to see her three-year-old lying on the kitchen floor. EMS was working on the boy who apparently had had a grand mal seizure. A number of neighbors were in the living room emotionally distraught. Entering the room, the mother rushed at me and thrust a Bible in my hand. "Here," she said, "you're a minister. Read something from the Bible!"

I appreciate the total panic that parents feel when their child's life is on the line. But, it does not work that way. You see, I am not Socrates, or Jesus, or Buddha. And even if I were any or all of them, there are times when words cannot fully describe or console the searing pain that people often feel in disease, trauma, divorce, betrayal, bankruptcy, and death.

The strength that scripture can give us follows years of spiritual discipline. Like God or Jesus, the Bible is not a fairy godmother that can grant your every wish when life becomes difficult and frightening. And the truth is, some people cannot hear those words, however well-intentioned they were uttered. I have learned that beyond the gentle greeting and embrace I can only say, "Let me just sit here with you for a while. I am not going to leave you alone."

One of the greatest fears that people express is dying alone. They are more afraid of dying alone than the death that will come from their cancer, or COPD, or end-stage renal failure. It reminds me of a story I heard a long time ago about a nurse who had a patient on her floor who was dying. He had no friends or family and had been in the hospital nearly two weeks without a single visitor.

As she was rounding near the end of her shift she noticed that the elderly man was weeping. She stepped into his room and asked, "Why the tears?"

He replied, "I don't want to die alone."

She answered, "You won't."

At the end of her shift the nurse clocked out. Returning to the patient's room, she scooted him over in his bed and laid down beside him. She slipped her left arm under his neck and brought him to her shoulder. Within a few minutes that man was sleeping gently. Early the next morning he died – in the presence of one who cared. I think that when Jesus said, "low I am with you always, even to the end of the age," that is the kind of presence he was talking about.

I am here for you – yes, even you.

Gary

The Chaplain's Chart – for the Week of May 9, 2016

You may recall that last Friday I attended a conference on quality care in hospitals with Francia Bird. As usual I was wearing my clerical collar. We were on our way to lunch when I was approached by a very small Asian woman. I would guess that she was in her sixties. She approached me and said, "Hello Fatta. How you doing?" I told her I was well, thanked her, and asked how she was doing. She beamed up at me and said, "I fine. You give me blessing?" She leaned into me. I put my left arm around her shoulder and my right hand on her head. I offered a prayer in the name of the Triune God. The lady crossed herself and said with a broad smile, "Oh, tank you Fatta." Little did she know that I was also blessed. I think the world, more than anything else, hungers for blessing.

In fact, you will not meet a human being today who does not need a blessing. A blessing does not require a clerical collar, or a Bible, or a religious symbol like a cross. Very often a gentle touch and a kind word is blessing enough. A blessing conveys the spirit of God to the other person, his or her needs, hopes, and fears. While the blessing originates with the Sacred One, it is conveyed by your voice and your hands. Whenever I meet a small child I put my hand on their head and whisper a prayer of grace for them. I will sometimes see a photograph of a person who has been killed or is starving to death on a city street. I put my fingers or hand on the image and offer a prayer.

Blessings are found in Jewish, Christian, Muslim, Hindu, and Buddhist traditions. It is not exclusive to any religion, denomination, or sect. Blessings are not the domain of men or women, clergy or laity. We can all be a blessing to others. We can all bless others. I am sure you are familiar with this Jewish blessing from Numbers 6:24:

"The LORD bless you and keep you;
25 The LORD make His face shine upon you,
And be gracious to you;
26 The LORD lift up His countenance upon you,
And give you peace."

This is the first stanza of a Buddhist healing blessing:

Just as the soft rains fill the streams,
Pour into the rivers and join together in the oceans,
So may the power of every moment of your goodness
Flow forth to awaken and heal all beings,
Those here now, those gone before, those yet to come.

A blessing can be as simple as, "I will hold you in my thoughts and prayers;" or "I am here for you." *Gary*

The Chaplain's Chart – for the Week of June 6, 2016

Every Sunday morning I offer "A Time for All Children," in our worship services in Hesston. Yesterday I was talking about thankfulness when one little boy said, "I never say 'thank-you.'"

I replied, "I'm sorry to hear that," and went on to talk about gratitude as the foundation of faith and spirituality. Thinking about anticipatory thanksgiving, I asked them what they were going to have for lunch and the boy's brother said, "We're going to grandma's house." He said she was preparing roast beef with mashed potatoes and gravy. I have eaten at her house and she is a marvelous cook.

The younger brother quipped, "I'd rather go to Sonic."

It turns out that this child suffers from a number of allergies and has a gluten free diet. He likes to go to Sonic because he can eat Sonic hotdogs, without the buns, of course. That's tough for an eight or nine year old kid to deal with. At the same time he has everything else in life that a little boy could hope for.

There was a sardonic tone in the boy's voice that was not only bitter but also arrogant. He will have to learn that everybody has issues and problems, and our response to life can only be, "THANK YOU!"

George Herbert, Anglican priest, author and poet wrote:

> Thou that hast given so much to me,
> Give one thing more – a grateful heart;
> Not thankful when it pleaseth me,
> As if Thy blessings had spare days;
> But such a heart, whose pulse may be
> Thy praise.

I witnessed grateful hearts in Emily's dance recital over the weekend. It was also the last recital for her very best friend, Randi. Randi graduated from high school and will be attending Wichita State University in the fall. She and Emily have danced together for the last eight years and have a bond more secure than the Federal Reserve. I watched their dancing in several group pieces but also a duet. They moved in graceful form, crying all the while. They wept

142

between sets. Yet they danced their hearts out, I think out of love and respect for one another. It was a hymn of joyful parting.

Several of the dance girls, their teachers, and parents came over to our house for a cookout after the Sunday performance. There was a great deal of chatter, a flurry of giggles, bouts of laughter, gift exchanges, hugs and kisses. One of the teachers, Andi, is a Type 1 diabetic. Andi has an insulin pump. She wears a lot of ink, her hair changes style and color every time I see her, and she sports a number of piercings. You would look at Randi and say, "Oh, yeah, she's a ballerina." You would look at Andi and think "bouncer" or "motorcycle chick." But Andi is one of the most gifted choreographers I have ever known. She is moving on to a teaching position in the Kansas City area. As she was leaving she gave me the usual bear hug, and said, "Thanks for everything."

No, thank you, Andi.

And many thanks to all of you. You have helped to form in me a grateful heart.

Gary

The Chaplain's Chart – for the Week of July 4, 2016

I often hear people say, "I have left it in God's hands." As Father Nathan Monk quipped, "You are God's hands," suggesting that we cannot walk away from our responsibilities to take care of ourselves, family, friends, and the planet. Similarly, I saw a post on Facebook that shows a surgeon talking with a man. He said something to the effect, "I'm sorry, but we were just two "Amens" away on Facebook to save your wife's life." I never respond to those kinds of posts or the "share" if you love Jesus, or America, or have the best wife/child/grandchild who ever walked the face of the earth. If I need Facebook to tell my wife/child/grandchild that I love them there is no real substance in the relationship to begin with.

Over the course of my ministry I have worked with all sorts of human needs and conditions and find myself saying over and over again, "It's all up to you," to attend AA, seek marital counseling or personal therapy, or make a choice about college, career change, or retirement. I cannot tell you the countless numbers of people who have asked me about spiritual growth but as soon as I show them disciplines such as the Daily Office, or Lectio Divina, or centering prayer I never hear from them again. They simply do not want to do the work.

I have angered more than one parishioner by saying, "I am not responsible for your faith. Only you are responsible for your faith. I may be responsible to your faith in terms of providing you with resources, guidance, and the discipline of love. But in the end your relationship with God is up to you."

It is not faith to "just trust in the Lord," but laziness. What my faith needs from God is the strength and courage to do what is expected of me; to sustain me in the peace of God's Holy Spirit; and to bend my heart toward wisdom that my actions are just and right. God may open doors, but we have to walk through them with the fullness of integrity and conscience. I think of Reinhold Niebuhr's "Serenity Prayer:"

> God grant me the serenity
> To accept the things I cannot change,
> Courage to change the things I can,
> And wisdom to know the difference.

I constantly remind people that I can know my relationship with God. I can know my relationship with them. But I cannot know their relationship with God. It is ultimate arrogance for me to think I know your relationship with the Sacred and dare to critique it or pass judgment on it.

Being mature adults and responsible for our lives and our relationships is hard work. It is not what most people want to hear. But it is the truth, and if we truly love and respect ourselves and others we will honor the labor of life and faith.

I believe in each and every one of you and I have no doubt that you are capable of great things.

Peace and Grace be with you all.

Gary

Throughout the Bible there are dozens of affirmations that God is with us. For example, consider this verse from Joshua 1:9, "Have I not commanded you? Be strong and courageous. Do not be frightened, and do not be dismayed, for the Lord your God is with you wherever you go." Or consider Isaiah 41:10, "Fear not, for I am with you; be not dismayed, for I am your God; I will strengthen you, I will help you, I will uphold you with my righteous hand." Jesus' name is Immanuel, "God with you." And Paul takes it a step further by declaring, "You are the body of Christ," suggesting that the Followers of the Way are the presence of God in the world. (I Corinthians 12:27)

So you should not be surprised when I tell you that I saw the Holy One working this past Friday. I have said this to you before, and it happens every day in different departments of our hospital throughout the day. But this particular incident happened in ICU. A young, 48-year-old patient with pancreatitis was struggling to live. He coded. His kidneys stopped working. It seemed to me that his body was shutting down. He needed dialysis but was too unstable to even transfer to a hospital that could provide it. You can also imagine that the family of such a young patient was in deep distress. All through the day, night, and into the next morning our team did everything possible to save the man's life. It was nearly twenty-four hours before he could be transferred. I understand that he coded on the way to Wichita, was revived again, but died a few hours later.

I watched the doctor, Sheila, Robin, Heather, Nathan, Jeff, Annette, and many others, I am sure, stand by the patient and work tirelessly to save his life. Do you understand that this is what it means when we say, "God is with us?" Teresa of Avila wrote, "Christ has no body now but yours. No hands, no feet on earth but yours. Yours are the eyes through which he looks compassion on this world. Yours are the feet with which he walks to do good. Yours are the hands through which he blesses all the world. Yours are the hands, yours are the feet, yours are the eyes, you are his body. Christ has no body now on earth but yours."

I do not think it matters much if you believe that Jesus is the

Christ. Your faith orientation may be completely different than mine. You may have a savior by a different name. It does not matter. When we engage such work as I have described, it is Holy Work – Sacred Work. It is the Source of all Life moving through our eyes, hands, minds, skills and feet creating, sustaining, and redeeming life.

I will never tire of telling you that the Holy One lives, moves, and has being in you. You are sacred vessels of mercy and healing.

Thank you one and all for the privilege of serving with you.
Chaplain Gary Blaine

The Chaplain's Chart – for the Week of July 25, 2016

Mimi and I call our little place Soggy Bottom, and boy is it soggy this morning with three and a quarter inches of rain in as many hours. There was a lot of water flowing over our country roads on my way to the hospital this morning.

We have a house and two out buildings. One is an old railroad car that we use as a horse barn, and the other is an old tractor barn where Emily parks her car and we keep tools and a canoe. Between these buildings there are probably six or eight Barn Swallow nests. Barn Swallows are a friend to farmers because they eat insects.

Barn Swallows mate for life. The couple builds their nest together, making about 1,000 trips to collect mud and straw or grass. The mud forms the foundation of the nest, followed by a mix of mud and grass or straw. The female will try to lay twice during the season. She will lay between two and eight eggs, though three or four seems most common. From what I have observed that is quite crowded. While she is sitting on her eggs the male will hunt food and feed her. After the eggs are hatched male and female are constantly flitting about collecting insects and feeding the hatchlings. The chicks sit in the nest with their mouths constantly open, impatiently waiting for the next deposit. I have watched one brood fly away and the second brood is laid in the same nest within a few days. A new nest has been built in the opposite corner and eggs are percolating there. Swallows will return to the same nest or nesting area year after year. Sometimes they will repair a nest or they will build a new one in the same place. If you knock their nest down they will come back to the same place next spring and start over.

I believe that Nature is the first revelation of God, and her creatures teach us many life lessons. The Barn Swallows offer a curricula on life together. The first tutorial is on fidelity. Working together these life mates build a home with all of the patience you could possibly imagine. I never heard a Barn Swallow say, "That's women's work," or "He never helps around the house." With loyalty to home, hearth, and young the Barn Swallows work tirelessly and without complaint.

Obviously building a nest and caring for young ones requires tremendous cooperation and coordination. They are industrious and go about the labor of life doing what needs to be done. There is no whining like, "Why do I have to get the mud?," or "You would all starve to death if I didn't get out there and catch those nasty flies and gnats." I don't know why humans always feel so put upon, as if God personally burdened them with doing the laundry or changing the cat litter.

And when all is said and done, the Barn Swallows leave the nest in flights of freedom and song. They will cluster on fence lines and chatter away, looking for a partner for the first time, and make their plans for a new nest and new life. Barn Swallows have a future because they make their future as soon as they step off their brooding nests and soar into the currents of Kansas wind.

I hope you have a splendid week.

Gary

The Chaplain's Chart – for the Week of August 8, 2016

The Mahatma Gandhi said, "The only devils in this world are the ones running around in our own hearts, and that is where all our battles should be fought." You can imagine that after 41 years of ministry in parishes, hospitals, institutions, and prisons, I have heard many people tell me about their battles with their friends, parents, and co-workers. And nearly every narrative that is told about these "devils" is never complete. They are almost always distorted, giving a very narrow perspective on the subject of their rage. They have worked on their story a very long time, being sure to highlight, if not exaggerate, the despicable qualities of their foe.

And I ask them, "Did he (or she) have no redeeming qualities? Was there nothing good about them? Did you never have a happy moment together?" They often look stunned for a moment. They seem confused because that was not a part of the narrative they had written and rehearsed so many times before they came to see me. I do not ask such things to convince them to stay in the relationship. I ask it because truth is essential to their healing.

Now certainly bad things happen to everybody. Every one of us can recall a family member, friend, roommate, spouse or ex-spouse, or co-worker who has treated us poorly, even abused us. They are accountable for their actions. Forgiveness and reconciliation are essential if the relationship is to have any kind of future. But the person who cut us so deeply is very often not the same "devil" that is running around in our hearts. The devil that is running around in our hearts bears some resemblance to the person who hurt us. Our anger, our fear, and our shame have blown that person out of perspective. We recast them into a demonic image while we give them powers and properties that were never there. The danger with these devils is that we begin to obsess about them and empower them with attributes for which there is no evidence.

Those are the real battles that must to be fought in our hearts and minds. I have fought such battles in the offices of a therapist, in the company of therapeutic friends and family, in a quiet room of a spiritual director, in prayer, and hundreds of hours in silent meditation. Long walks in mountains and subtle moments in streams and rivers are powerfully restorative. But those are only the tools of the heart. The work of the heart is releasing the anger and bitterness, the exaggeration and distortion that we have given to these people or situations. The work of the heart is finding your true self, free from the bondage and shackles of rage and despair.

That does not mean that marriages or families or friendships will be salvaged. For just as much as we need to fight the devils in our own hearts so will our parents, spouses, friends, children, and co-workers need to fight theirs.

In the Anglican *Book of Common Prayer,* we read, "we have

left undone those things we ought to have done, and we have done those things which we ought not to have done." Perhaps we should refine our confession to say, "and we have given free reign to the devils that are running around in our own hearts."

I hope you will think about this. Such battles are burdensome and require a lot from us. But if we let the devils run around it will cripple us spiritually and emotionally. I don't think God means for us to live so disabled.

Gary

The Chaplain's Chart – for the Week of August 29, 2016

Do you ever find yourself in a situation that you had promised yourself you would never get into again? Several years ago I officiated at a wedding in a city park in Tulsa. It was a hot, sweltering August evening. The temperature was 105 degrees. The groom and groomsmen were wearing black tuxedos and I was dressed in my usual clerical garb. The mother of the groom was almost an hour late, long enough for everyone to broil.

Like many parks there were gravel paths, walkways of woodchips, and several little streams that flowed into a pond. The ring bearer, about four years of age, was running around with the ring pillow and the actual ring sewed lightly onto the pillow. I suggested to the bridal party they keep the ring until the ceremony started. They were certain everything would be fine. By five o'clock everyone finally showed up and we were able to begin the ceremony. Everybody was drenched in sweat. And you guessed it, the ring was nowhere to be found. We broke up for a few minutes trying to remember where we had seen the ring bearer, and with him the ring. When we finally found him the ring was gone!

I made a vow that I would never do an outdoor wedding in the summer again.

But guess what I was doing Saturday evening at 6:30? The temperature was about 90 degrees and the humidity was pretty high. The sun had begun to lower behind the house, giving the guests some shade. The bride and groom had their backs to the sun. But I stood there, looking straight into the fiery eyes of Helios. In no time at all I began to sweat. About a third of the way into the ceremony sweat started running into my eyes, stinging like crazy. The bride gave me her kerchief and I was able to dab my eyes. But the kerchief had some kind of perfume on it, stinging my eyes even more and making my nose run. It got so bad I had to close my left eye completely.

My grandfather used to say that if a dog bites you the first time it's his fault. If he bites you a second time it's your fault. So, I am bit a second time and I vow to never do an outdoor summer wedding again; at least not until someone I care about really wants one and I cannot negotiate a different time of year or an indoor wedding.

We get ourselves in difficult situations not just because we are dumb, but also because we mean to do good things for people and we want to make them happy. What I experienced in both weddings could not be classified as "suffering." They were uncomfortable, to be sure. They were inconvenient. But everyone survived, had a good time, and now have stories to tell their families and friends. Hopefully the bride and groom will enjoy many years of joy.

Caring for people, at the very least, is often problematic. But there is no comparison to the hope and happiness we might give to someone else. Just remember to bring your own pocket handkerchief the next time.

I am here for you and hope you have a great week.
Gary

The Chaplain's Chart – for the Week of September 5, 2016

September is Suicide Awareness and Prevention month. The C.D.C. defines suicide as death caused by self-directed injurious behavior with an intent to die as a result of the behavior. A suicide attempt is a nonfatal, self-directed potentially injurious behavior with the intent to die. Men continue to lead the number of suicides in the United States, but women's rates are markedly climbing. The adjusted rate of suicide between 1999 and 2014 has increased 24%. Sadly, suicide has increased 150% amongst veterans since

2001. The rate of suicide in Kansas rose 30% in the last two years. And, not coincidently, the budget for mental health services has dropped 30% in the same period of time. The preferred method of suicide is by firearms, though hanging is rapidly rising, followed by "poisoning," i.e. overdose.

There are several myths about suicide. (1) People who talk about suicide won't really do it. – In fact, almost everyone who commits or attempts suicide has given some kind of verbal clue. (2) Anyone who tries to kill him or herself must be crazy. – Most suicidal people are not psychotic, though they most likely suffer from depression. (3) If a person is determined to kill him or herself, nothing can stop them. – More than half of suicide victims have sought help in the six months prior to death. (4) Talking about suicide may give someone the idea to kill themselves. – The exact opposite is true. You cannot give the suicidal person morbid ideas by talking about suicide. They have already been thinking about or planning it. Let me rephrase that: Talking about suicide doesn't hurt anyone – not talking about it does.

Risk factors for suicide include, most commonly, depression. Depression is often undiagnosed and untreated. Other factors include alcoholism and drug abuse, previous suicide attempts or a family history of suicide, terminal illness and chronic pain, social isolation and loneliness (a huge issue for elders and teens), trauma and abuse. Suicide factors for teens also include physical and sexual abuse. A hostile school environment and bullying is a common risk for adolescent suicide. The availability of guns is a risk factor for all ages, but especially for teens.

Suicide has many warning signs, including suicidal ideation. Suicide ideation includes comments like, "I wish I hadn't been born;" "If I see you again;" "I'd be better off dead;" "I have no reason to live;" "I am just a burden to everybody." Another warning sign is searching for ways to kill oneself, which leads to the purchase of guns, or stockpiling narcotic drugs, or searching online for methods of suicide. Suicidal people often increase their use of alcohol or drugs. Some people who are planning to kill themselves will get their affairs in order, including last will and testament or funeral directions. Giving away personal possessions can also be a warning sign of suicide. Irritability and withdrawal from others often indicates a potential suicide. But there are many who become very calm and peaceful before they kill themselves. They have made up their minds and prepared everything for their deaths.

How can we respond to someone who is expressing the signs of suicide?

> If you are worried, speak up. "I noticed that you are not yourself these days and I just wanted to check in with you." "How can I support you right now?" "You are not alone in this. I am here for you." Whatever you do, do not argue, act shocked, or promise secrecy. Be yourself and be open. Offer to help.

> Utilize the National Suicide Prevention hotline at 1-800-273-8255. They will direct you to a local intervention team. If the person is in the act of suicide call 911.

> MY3 app is available for both Android and Apple users, free of charge. MY3 has you identify three people you can reach out to when you are feeling suicidal. Its Safety Plan includes self-chosen activities that direct you to those things that help you relax and reduce anxiety. This might be as simple as taking a walk or swimming, crocheting, yoga, meditation, or drawing.

Suicide is preventable and you have taken the first step by reading this article. Connecting, communicating, and caring are the fundamental ingredients in suicide prevention.

As ever, I am here for you.
Chaplain Gary Blaine

The Chaplain's Chart – for the Week of September 12, 2016

When I think of all the things that I do as a chaplain and pastor, I realize it is the little things that matter. So, on any one given day I might round in the emergency department three or four times, convene a Palliative Care Team meeting and write recommendations, respond to codes, visit patients, offer the sacraments and help families make decisions for hospice, nursing homes, or memorial arrangements. In my church I prepare and deliver sermons, teach an adult Sunday school class, and visit the hospitalized. For both church and hospital I officiate at baptisms, weddings, and memorial services. I also engage in pastoral counseling in both settings.

Despite all of this, and their seeming importance at the time, it is the little things that really count. When someone in the church has major surgery and manages to get back home I make chicken soup for them and take them a loaf of my fresh baked bread and a jar of homemade preserves. That is what they remember, not the prayers, or rites, or counsel.

Last Wednesday I set out the comfort carts. Thursday afternoon I realized that all but one of the comfort stones in the third floor waiting room had been taken. That is fine, they are welcome to take them home. I replenished the supply and was standing at the elevator when two women approached me.

"Are you the one responsible for these?" one of them asked, pulling a stone out of her pocket.

I told her I was and she then asked, "Well how long have you been doing that."

"About 24 hours," I answered.

"Oh, thank you so much," she said. "They bring me so much comfort and joy."

Her companion agreed and the woman went on to tell me that her father carried a stone in his pocket that he gathered from a favorite lake. He kept it in his pocket until the day he died and the woman got to keep it. She told me that there was actually a little indentation that he had worn into the stone.

Who would have thought that a polished stone with words like "Hope," "Inspire," "Faith," and "Love," would give people so much serenity? Of course, it is not the stone that does it, but something to hold on to that points us to higher values and inspiration.

It is the simple things like a slow meal with friends and neighbors, a quiet time of reflection under a tree, the sound of rushing water over a dam, the gentle patter of rain on the roof that ground us to what is real. Such things demand little or nothing of us.

Nineteenth century Shakespearian actor, Edwin Booth, (no, it was his brother that shot president Lincoln) wrote, "When you are older you will understand how precious little things, seemingly of no value in themselves, can be loved and prized above all price when they convey the love and thoughtfulness of a good heart."

May you be flooded by oceans of little things this week. If that doesn't happen, come and see me and we will have a good cup of coffee together and hold gentle conversation.

Much love to all of you. *Gary*

The Chaplain's Chart – for the Week of September 19, 2016

I cannot think of a more cherished value in the Bible than hospitality. Beyond Judaism and Christianity, hospitality is the hallmark of many religions and cultures around the globe. Hospitality remains a valued characteristic of people, families, and communities in just about every place I can think of. In the first century of the Common Era a visitor was greeted by servants who washed your feet and rubbed them with healing oils spiced with fragrances such as frankincense or myrrh. Guests were given plenty of good food and drink, comfortable accommodations for the night's stay, and food for their journey the next day. Failure to extend hospitality was considered a social *faux pas* and brought down shame and scorn on you and your household. Every family must be prepared to offer hospitality at any time of any day.

Most of us can fulfill the duties of hospitality for an evening, let's say a meal with your neighbors, or Sunday dinner with your family. But what if someone comes and stays over a week? A week's worth of hospitality gets to be expensive and tries your patience. For example, they drink more beer in a day than you do in a month. They put everything in the wrong place in the kitchen cabinets, such as measuring cups with the glasses, cooking utensils with the eating utensils, and mixing bowls with the pots and pans. They brush their teeth at the kitchen sink, despite the fact that you have two bathrooms, and floss their teeth at the dining room table when you are have trying to have a conversation. Life on a small farm is like living on the Ponderosa to them and they want to help

154

with feeding the animals. Of course they forget to close gates, allowing a chicken to get out and be served up to your neighbor's dog.

Hospitality requires you to listen to their endless chatter about issues you have absolutely no interest in discussing. By the end of the second day your ears hurt. When they leave everyone in your family scatters to their own silent space, grabs a favorite book and pulls their blankets up to their noses. The house is as quiet as a public library at three o'clock in the morning and the understood message is "Quiet! Please!" The dogs quit shivering and the cats reappear from under the bed or closet.

Of course it is through hospitality that we get caught up on family news such as your sister who has moved to Louisiana but no one knows where. In fact, we don't even know if she is alive or not. The daughter who got married and only sent you a text after the fact. Then there are all of the wonderful things they did around the house like installing a battery powered backup sump pump in the basement, mowing the lawn, and mucking out the barn. It's funny that visitors think mucking the barn is a real adventure. Hospitality allows them the fantasy that they now know everything there is to know about country living.

In the ancient world hospitality was an essential means of safe travels and provision for the journey. I think it is still important for getting us all down the road of life. Yes, it is expensive and inconvenient. But hospitality may be the last bastion against hostility in a world of egotism, bigotry, isolationist thinking, and flat out fear of others.

Safe travels to you all this week. Stop by our place any time. We might have a beer or two left to share with you.
Chaplain Gary Blaine

The Chaplain's Chart – for the Week of September 26, 2016

I was in a great deal of pain on Sunday, a week ago, even though I had taken some pain medication. Preparing a meal for eight, including some fresh baked French bread, I sat at my place at the table quite spent. As our guests were leaving, Mary bent over my chair. Her cheeks were close to mine and I could feel her hair against my face. She whispered to me, "I am so sorry you are so uncomfortable. If there is anything I can do for you, just ask."

I have known Mary for seven or eight years. She is, in my mind, a beautiful young woman. Mary excels in handcrafts and is now studying interior design. She will surpass her classmates in that, I have no doubt. But she is also a hunter with bow and rifle. More than that, she dresses out her meat and butchers it for freezing. We have enjoyed several venison roasts and ground meat from her butcher's block. Mary prepares her meat in her own garage because she thinks that most slaughter houses in the area waste too much meat. Mary is also an accomplished equestrian.

The burden that I carry with Mary is the deep psychological neglect and even abuse that her mother has punished her with all of her life. The mother refused to go to Mary's wedding, has belittled her since childhood, and will tell Mary about a family event that happened a week ago to which Mary and her family were not invited. She once told Mary that she had sold her horse, even though she had actually hidden it on a relative's farm. Mary and I have had several long and quiet conversations and I have tried to tell her, "This is not about you. This is all about your mother and her own deep seated pathology. Her cruelty is not a reflection on the wonderful person that you are."

But it is hard to feel cherished when your own mother has forsaken you since childhood. Yet, somehow, Mary is rising above it. Her gesture to me last week was nothing less than sacred. From her own wounded heart she offered profound empathy for another human being. I felt blessed and still wonder at the movement of grace Mary tendered me.

Every human being that you and I will meet every day of our lives has a carpetbag of pain, abuse, neglect, anxiety and fear that they carry with them. I do not think that any of us can escape that. I assume that about every person I meet and try to be kind to them. With the grace of God I can carry that baggage with them, at least for a little while, maybe a few miles down the road.

You will be surprised how many of those same wounded healers can also carry you. They will blush against your heart with

156

the most unexpected and authentic words of hope. You see, God is with us and touches us with whispered words and gentle palpations. Even the broken heart is a hand and voice of healing.

May your burdens be light this week and your eyes and ears ever open to the pain of others. I am still here for you.

Gary

The Chaplain's Chart – for the Week of October 3, 2016

The weekend really began on Thursday with "Taste of Newton" where I enjoyed blueberry cobbler cooked in a Dutch oven by the Boy Scouts. Emily danced a solo point piece. I thought she did a great job, especially considering the fact that she was on asphalt. She always uses an older pair of point shoes because they are absolutely ruined on street surfaces. Emily, of course, is her own harshest critic and would later point out a dozen flaws in her performance.

Emily is the most unique of all my children. She has an artist's soul and that is difficult to navigate. I have learned to give her mind a large stage to act out her life. From what I can tell, men do not occupy much of her consciousness, and that is just fine with me. On the ground floor of our house I can look down the stairwell to the basement and see her feet. They will move across the dance floor and then stop to scurry over to a table where she marks the choreography she is developing. The music is backed up and she starts over. There is a lot of repetition and I should think it is sometimes tedious. But that is her art and she is totally dedicated to developing her skill set.

When she is not at dance or school, you can find her in our craft room making cards or gifts for friends and family. Cooking is also one of her activities, especially from recipes she downloads from Pinterest. Yesterday she made pumpkin spice cookies with a cream cheese frosting.

I have said many times that when we found out that Mimi was pregnant I was fifty years of age. I thought to myself, "I'm not sure I have enough energy for this." But every day of her life is a blessing to me and I am so grateful for the privilege of sharing the stage with her—even if now I am increasingly working behind the scenes. The day will come when my role will be mostly that of audience.

Now don't get me wrong. All of my children are special and I love them. One son is a Pilate's instructor, another is in law school, and the last is a bank manager. My other daughters include a bank employee and my oldest daughter works for the State of Florida in health and human services. She has risen quite far and fast and has tremendous leadership responsibilities.

What is really different? Me. After I realized that I was never going to be a bishop, and that churches are like giant sponges that will soak up your very life blood, I decided I had put my priorities in the wrong place. With Emily I decided that I would spend more time with her. So, for example, I made Mondays my day off and spent the day with her until she entered kindergarten. I made it a point to attend as many recitals and performances as possible. Mimi and I have spared no expense for her dance training and college preparation.

It is one thing to count your blessings. It is quite another to develop and nurture the blessings that have been given to you.

I know that sometimes you might think that words I use in reference to you, such as, "I am here for you," are just the words a chaplain is supposed to say. But I would like for you to know that those words come from the depths of my soul. Because, you see, you are a blessing too.

Chaplain Gary Blaine

The Chaplain's Chart – for the Week of October 10, 2016

Go back with me in history 2,600 years ago. The Jewish people had lost Jerusalem to the power of Babylon. Jewish leadership, including religious, political, legal, social, and commercial, were forced out of Jerusalem and held in captivity in Babylon. They had lost nearly everything, including their property, wealth, and place in society. Meanwhile, the prophet Jeremiah remained in the city of Jerusalem. He wrote them a letter telling the Jews to build houses, plant gardens and enjoy the fruits and vegetables of their gardens, have sons and daughters and bless them with their own marriages and children. And not only that, but "seek the welfare of the city where I have sent you into exile." (Jeremiah 29:4-9)

So let's get this straight. In the midst of tremendous personal and social loss, God not only expects us to prosper but also to seek the welfare of the very people who inflicted so much pain and grief upon us.

We have all heard it said, "Living well is the best revenge." But Jeremiah takes this to a much deeper and broader level. His letter from God is basically an invitation to let your life and your lifestyle be the greatest protest that you can make in an atmosphere of oppression. AND, lift your oppressor to new levels of welfare.

This is as radical a way of thinking in the ancient world as I can think of. It is as radical a way of thinking in the modern world as I can think of. Jeremiah is not seeking revenge, or "an eye for an eye," or "shock and awe." He is saying that in the midst of calamity rebuild your life with as much grace and style as you possibly can. Let your new fortunes bless the entire community where you live.

The same thing applies to ourselves and our patients. With the news of a new chronic disease or even a diagnosis of a terminal disease, go home and rebuild your house and plant your garden. Bless your family, your friends, your faith community, and your city. That includes those who have just been served with divorce papers, or pink slips, or retirement, bankruptcy, or the news that your teenaged daughter is pregnant, addicted to methamphetamine and in the local hoosegow.

This is how we return to the beloved City of Jerusalem – the city of peace – the city of wholeness.

Nothing falls out of the sky and does the work of home building, gardening, and nurturing families. The work of restoration is in our hands and it starts wherever we are and regardless of the circumstances. It is hard work and seldom is it recognized and appreciated. But that is the path of transformation. There is no victimization here, no one to get even with. Besides, you won't have time for that kind of foolishness. You have gutters to clean, the last of the tomatoes to can, and sitting with your granddaughter later in the day. Sunday is family dinner at your house and there is bread to bake and gifts to wrap.

Yours in deepest faith, in you and all that is Sacred,
Chaplain Gary Blaine

The Chaplain's Chart – for the Week of October 24, 2016

Licking tongues of light flit out across the horizon, making harvest colors a golden bronze. The Kansas breezes whisper over the plains. A rooster crows in the distance and the Mocking bird warms up for a morning of vocal gymnastics. It imitates the Blue Jay, the Red Cardinal, and then yodels the last song it heard before sleep.

There are times when we have to turn off the television, the computer, and the smart phone. We have to step out on the front porch to listen to the early voices of the Creation. From the poem "Some Days," by Philip Terman, we read:

> "You have to close all the books and open
> all the windows so that whatever swirls
> inside can leave and whatever flutters
> against the glass can enter."

In my experience this is as necessary as drinking, eating, working, and exercising. We have to "air out," as the common expression states it. That also means no tablets, computers, phones, or even bills to pay. We have to let out all the chaos created by all of the voices that pummel us with responsibilities, things to do, and expectations. We have to let all that dust blow out of our minds and hearts and allow the fresh air to get it. While all of the cobwebs of mental and spiritual fatigue are whooshed away, fresh perspectives from the dawn of creation inspire us to new possibilities. Sometimes they simply leave us with a sense of cleanliness.

The other day I talked with a man who was dying. Both he and his wife were at peace with this growing reality, after the initial protests of denial. How does this happen? It happens because they have spent time growing the perspective that birth, life, and death are part of the entire package that God gives us all. It happens, I'll wager, because they have spent plenty of time on their front porch, or a mountain stream, or a vista in the Flint Hills watching the sun go down.

I often hear people say, "Chaplain, that sounds great. I have got to start doing that. But I just can't seem to find the time." And those are the souls I worry about because those are the souls that get burned out, easily fatigued, and caught off guard by crises of one kind or another. Their souls are so congested with old worries, nonsense, and unresolved issues that they have no reserves to fight the necessary battles of life or confront new challenges.

Please understand that I simply do not mean "my alone time." It is a discipline of emptying our hearts and minds so that the light of God can enter in. Sometimes God is "whatever flutters against the glass," and we must take the time to open the windows.

May the Spirit of God flutter against your windows this week.   *Chaplain Gary Blaine*

The Chaplain's Chart – for the Week of October 31, 2016

Last Tuesday morning I went with Mimi to the veterinarian's office. We brought in our dog, "Doc." Doc had been diagnosed with liver cancer a few months ago and now he could not stand up. The vet thought that the cancer had spread to his spine.

Mimi and Emily rescued Doc from an animal shelter. During the last few months of his life Mimi prepared special meals for Doc and even hand fed him to keep him nourished. She did not want him to die alone at the vet's, so we became a kind of pet hospice at home.

Tuesday evening about 8:15 the phone rang. It was Emily telling us she had been in an automobile accident. In fact, she totaled her car. Fortunately no one was injured. As I was talking with her on the phone I said to her, "Emily, the most important thing is that you are not hurt." She started crying.

I later asked her why she cried and she told me, "Because you were so kind to me. Your voice got really soft when you told me the most important thing was that I was OK."

Now, please understand, I don't think I have ever even raised my voice with Emily in the last 17 years and eleven months. I have always spoken to her with the utmost love and respect. So why would she be surprised or taken aback when I did not get angry or rude with her?

I'm sure that like a lot of kids she thought, "My parents are going to kill me." But more importantly, when any of us are hurt, or in trouble we melt before the loving voice and the gentle touch. Kindness often disarms fear and anxiety. In the face of loving kindness we do not need to be defensive. Loving kindness even dispels hate, so said the Buddha.

You will never meet another human being – any day for the rest of your life – who has not had accidents, been injured, faced setbacks and defeats or disappointed themselves and others. You will never meet another human being – any day for the rest of your life – who is not hungry for a word or gesture of compassion

Kindness is the order of the day as we start an IV on a child who is kicking and screaming; or the embarrassed elder who has lost bowel control; or the frightened patient who just learned they have a fatal disease. I cannot think of any situation in the hospital, both in terms of patient care and employee relationships, where kindness is not needed.

The heart of all religion is essentially loving kindness toward others, speaking the truth with compassion, and doing the right thing. It's as simple – and as hard – as that.

Now let me make a confession. Whenever you say "Hi Chaplain," or pat me on the back or give me a hug I feel valued and loved. It reminds me of why I come to work at S.B.A. Memorial Hospital every day.

May love and gentleness follow you all the days of your lives. *Chaplain Gary Blaine*

The Chaplain's Chart – for the Week of November 21, 2016

G. K. Chesterton wrote, "When it comes to life, the critical thing is whether you take things for granted or take them with gratitude." Did you know there is a relationship between gratitude and health? And by health I mean physical, emotional, spiritual, mental, moral, and social health. Harvard Medical School reports, "In positive psychology research, gratitude is strongly and consistently associated with greater happiness. Gratitude helps people feel more positive emotions, relish good experiences, improve their health, deal with adversity, and build strong relationships." (Harvard Health Publications, November, 2011)

Gratitude comes from the Latin, *gratia,* meaning grace or gratefulness. You might also recognize it in the Italian *grazi,* or the Spanish, *gracias.* When we recognize the grace in our lives we cannot help but say, "Thank you," or "I am so grateful." Most of the time such grace comes from beyond ourselves or the making of our own hands. Gratitude unites us with the source of that grace, whether it comes from friends, family, work, nature, or the Source of all life. When the Pilgrims sat down for their first "Thanksgiving" feast it was in recognition that their bellies were full and their stores were laid by for the winter. All of that is due to the grace of God at the hands of Native Americans who taught them how to plant the three sisters – corn, beans, and squash – in mounds of earth fertilized by fish; how to hunt beaver; and where the best places were to hunt fowl and fish. They also taught them how to identify beneficial and toxic plants and berries.

Gratitude is a marked characteristic in patients who recover more quickly from surgery or illness and who die more peacefully. In a 2006 study published in *Behavior Research and Therapy,* Vietnam veterans who had higher levels of gratitude experienced lower rates of Post-Traumatic Stress Disorder. Gratitude may not prevent chronic diseases but it can help navigate us through them.

Gratitude is not just an attitude or something we can make up when the mood strikes us. Gratitude is a daily practice that we cultivate, and in the cultivation we find ourselves with a deep appreciation for our lives and all of the gifts within our daily experience. I knew a man who made it a practice to write four "thank you" cards a day to friends and colleagues.

Writing thank you notes is something all of us can do. It just has to be a few sentences to let someone know how much you appreciate them. Ann Voskamp's book, *1000 Gifts,* teaches us how to keep a gratitude journal. Some families keep a small box on the dining room table for family members to write a thank you note throughout the week and drop it in the box. At the end of the week all of the notes are read aloud at the dinner table. Offering thanks before meals is an essential discipline, even if it is a silent prayer in a busy restaurant. Giving thanks in the morning for the blessing of a new day, and at the end of the day for all the blessings received enlightens our hearts.

English poet, John Milton, wrote, "Gratitude bestows reverence, allowing us to encounter everyday epiphanies, those transcendent moments of awe that change forever how we experience life and the world."

May your Thanksgiving Day be filled with reverence and awe.

Chaplain Gary Blaine

The Chaplain's Chart – for the Week of December 12, 2016

In his hope that Israel would be restored, the prophet Isaiah wrote, "The wilderness and the dry land shall be glad, the desert shall rejoice and blossom, like the crocus it shall blossom abundantly, and rejoice with joy and singing." Such is the hope for Christians in this season of Advent. In the midst of the wilderness a new hope shall blossom abundantly.

Isaiah's use of the crocus as a metaphor is both subtle and beautiful. There are ninety species of the crocus, a small flowering plant with a variety of gentle colors. They are white, orange, violet and many more. The crocus blooms in the spring, summer, and fall. Wilderness in the Old Testament very closely resembles our word desert. It has little rainfall and is, therefore, dry, rocky, and often barren. Isaiah dares to claim that in the midst of this fairly hostile and seemingly uninhabitable landscape, a beautiful flower will bloom. Such is the kingdom of God.

The crocus is a small plant and you have to know how to look for it and to see it. With the heat of the sun and wind and sand blowing in our faces we could easily miss the crocus. Such is the kingdom of God. I have been very blessed this past week to see the crocus.

164

My son, Jeremy, sent me a picture of my granddaughter, Scotland Jane, asleep on his chest. He wrote, "What a great way to spend Saturday afternoon." I replied that this is one of the sacred memories of my life, my infant children asleep on my chest. Now that's a crocus. I also received a note last week from my dear friend, Kay Northcutt, which was stuffed with love, joy, and hope. I have been praying her letter since December 7th. Another crocus.

I fear that our nation is becoming like the wilderness. There is much that is dry, hard, brittle, uninhabitable, and inhospitable. I am speaking of the desert gale winds of prejudice, fear, greed, anger, and division. I am speaking of the tremendous rise of hate crimes since the election on November 8, with swastikas painted on synagogues and mosques, and the homes of Muslims. People are assaulted because they wear a hijab or a turban or the color of their skin is different. I am also speaking of the 45 million people who still live in poverty, and the 33 million who are not insured and thus receive inadequate health care. The FBI reported last year that there are tens of thousands of children who were sexually exploited in the United States.

It is in the midst of such wilderness that I look for the crocus because I believe that we cannot live without hope. I dare hold onto the faith that God is with us, regardless of the terrain we live in and struggle with. But here is an even bigger challenge – to be a crocus in the lives of people I meet every day. John Mark Green wrote, "Hope is a flower which refuses to be crushed under life's brutal heel." Sounds too sentimental? Try living without those subtle messages of hope that God continues to deliver through the most unassuming crocus.

Bloom where you are planted today and you will be surprised when someone stops on their desert journey, falls to their knees and says, "Oh, thank you. I think I can go on from here."

Chaplain Gary Blaine

Isabel Currier was an author whose works appeared in *The New Yorker.* Currier wrote, "It is the personal thoughtfulness, the warm human awareness, the reaching out of the self to one's fellow man that makes giving worthy of the Christmas spirit." Thoughtfulness, the warm human awareness, and the reaching out of the self to others is, indeed, the essence of the season we call Christmas. And one can only hope that such human gifting flows out of this seasonal celebration to touch the hearts of human beings throughout the year and around the world. As such it is not the lone purview of Christianity, but the hope of every human being that I know of.

The giving of self to others is perhaps one of the most important exercises of the human heart, mind, and soul. Research shows us that people who have an opportunity to give to others consistently find greater value in the act of giving than in the act of receiving. Giving is more than searching online for a gift at Amazon. It involves thoughtfulness about the person we are buying for, their age, gender, interests, and passions. When we can give the present personally we get to see their expressions of surprise, joy, and thankfulness. If we are lucky we even get a heartfelt hug. When we make these kinds of efforts we are demonstrating a level of empathy and appreciation that is far greater than the cost of the gift. It also further binds us to one another, even if the gift itself is not exactly what the person had in mind.

The simple joy and peace of mind that giving brings to our health is very much like the effectiveness of gardening. Nursing homes and some hospitals have therapeutic gardens where residents and patients can plant and grow living things. We know that such projects relieve tension and lower blood pressure. Hesston Community Child Care gathers at Schowalter Villa, a retirement center. Young children, college students, and elders have opportunities to garden, craft, celebrate holidays, and share food, stories and songs. In a word, they are giving themselves to each other. For some of the residents this becomes an essential purpose for their lives. For some of the children they are given the gift of love that only a grandparent can share.

Phillips Brooks was an American Episcopal bishop in the 19th century. You remember him as the author of *O Little Town of Bethlehem*. Bishop Brooks wrote, "The earth has grown old with its burden of care. But at Christmas it always is young." In this 21st century the burdens of the earth are heavy indeed. I wonder that we do not break under the weight of poverty, violence, greed, and extreme hatred. I believe that the world will be a better place not in the making of more things but in the giving of self; not in the making of deals or even treaties but in the sharing of our hearts with one another; not in political or economic schemes but in the exchange of mutual love, warm human awareness and respect.

If it is true health that we want for ourselves, our children, and our neighbors around the world, let us give ourselves away. Wouldn't that be a remarkable Christmas?

May yours be a joyful Christmastide.
Chaplain Gary Blaine

The Chaplain's Chart – for the Week of February 6, 2017

You have heard it said that music is the universal language. I believe that is true. Music certainly has its regional and cultural characteristics but those can cross many borders and ethnicities. Even if the words do not sync with our theology the melody lifts us above the rigors of creed and doctrine.

Yesterday we sang "Jesus Lover of My Soul." That is a common hymn in evangelical protestant churches. I have sung it most of my life. But I didn't really hear it until I attended the funeral of a black Methodist emeritus minister in his home church. He was more than "superannuated" as the Methodists call it. Superannuated is an old term to describe the elderly and retired. It also means old fashioned, antiquated, broken down, and **very** old. We sang the last stanza *a cappella*. The other hymn was, "On Jordan's Stormy Banks I Stand," offered in the full strength of that hope, with a powerful choir and instrumentation. They held nothing back. And I am convinced the force of that music catapulted that old black preacher into realms beyond this earth.

I was transported by this experience. It carried me to sweeping heights I had never known in music, save a live performance of Beethoven's Ninth Symphony, the last movement, "Ode to Joy." In these experiences I was taken out of myself and blended into the soul of the music, with its rhythm, melody, harmony, timbre, and texture. It transformed me. I am never the same after such an experience.

I learned a long time ago that music brings balance to a worship service. When I have worked with gifted musicians we talk about the mood and feeling of the service and I look to them to provide the balance. If a sermon is deep and requires a lot of thought or soul searching, I want the music to be uplifting. If a sermon is more on the "inspirational side," I want the music to bring some gravity to the worship experience. I also know that I can preach a decent sermon and the music and hymnody kills the spirit and mood of what I have offered. Powerful music can offset a weak sermon. And there is nothing that can kill a worship service right out of the box than a prelude that sounds like the breathy organ music of a funeral parlor.

Music is very important to my own spiritual well-being and my professional responsibilities. I like a variety of musical genres from classical to blues, folk, and rock. I love to sing, not only on Sunday mornings, but also in the car. This Tuesday evening Mimi and I will attend a concert at Bethel College by Ladysmith Black Mambazo. I first heard them on Paul Simon's album, "Graceland." Their *a cappella* rendition of "Homeless" still lifts my heart.

I encourage every spiritual discipline to include music. Listen to it, sing with it, and dance your heart out. Music is the gift of God for all souls who want to be thrilled, soothed, healed, converted, and encouraged. Music is the voice of gratitude.

Sing away!
Chaplain Gary Blaine

The Chaplain's Chart – for the Week of February 13, 2017

I am worried about you!
I am very aware that since about Thanksgiving we

have maintained a consistent and high patient census. In many departments some employees are working fifty hours a week or more. The fatigue is evident in your faces, your attitudes, and sometimes in your interactions with other people. PLEASE do not hear that as confrontational or judgmental. I get it. I understand that fatigue first starts in the body but quickly erodes our minds, emotions, and souls.

The hospital administration is working hard to address this situation with a full court press to bring staffing relief. And you know that takes time in terms of recruiting and orienting.

So it seems to me that each and every one of us must stop and ask about our own self-care. Self-care means YOU have to take care of YOU. It is just like my diabetes. Even the people who love me the most, like Mimi, cannot exercise for me, take my medications, or comply with a diabetic diet.

But let's begin by looking at some of the signs of stress.

✓ **Physical:** Nausea, chest pain, difficulty breathing, headaches, grinding of teeth, weakness, elevated blood pressure, rapid heart rate, diarrhea or constipation.
✓ **Cognitive:** Blaming others, confusion, poor attention, poor concentration, heightened or lowered alertness, poor problem solving – can't make decisions.
✓ **Emotional:** Anxiety or panic, fear, uncertainty, depression, feeling overwhelmed, anger, irritability, unspecified grief, weeping, loss of emotional control.
✓ **Behavioral:** Change in normal routines, withdrawal, unhealthy alcohol or drug consumption, somatic complaints, pacing, intensified startle reflex, change in sexual function, inability to rest or relax, suspiciousness or lack of trust.
✓ **Spiritual:** anger with God, withdrawal of spiritual practices or rituals, withdrawal from your faith community or uncharacteristic involvement with your faith community, anger with clergy, loss of moral compass, **loss of meaning or purpose.** Despair or existential malaise.

Here are some things to try:

- Physical exercise – even if only taking a 30 minute walk every day.
- Rest or engage in peaceful activities such as crafting, painting, dancing.
- Talk to people who will listen deeply. Spend quality time with friends and family – eating out, picnics, game nights.
- Yoga.
- Meditation such as silent meditation or centering prayer or Mantram repetition.
- Keep a journal especially of dreams, ideas, even hopes and concerns.
- Do things that feel good to you, reward you, and affirm you.
- Eat well balanced meals and snacks.
- If necessary find professional help, or talk with your minister/priest/chaplain.
- DRINK LOTS OF WATER!!!

As I have long said, I am here for you. Conversations that we have are strictly confidential, and I live to serve you. Be whole and know that I love you. *Chaplain Gary Blaine*

The Chaplain's Chart – for the Week of March 6, 2017

I don't know about you but I am a little concerned about what the weather will do next. My peach and apple trees have buds on them. The same thing happed the last two years. They were wiped out by a killing frost in late March.

My horses started shedding their winter coats about three weeks ago. They have never shed in February before. We desperately need rain. The winter wheat is turning yellow again and the big topic of conversation at church yesterday was wind, rain, and fire.

We can spend every waking hour worrying about "what if." We see patients who are absolutely petrified because they have had a TIA ('mini stroke') and live alone, or just been diagnosed with cancer, or had their first heart attack. The problem is that many of us have lived long enough to know that things can go wrong, despite out best safe-guards and precautions. I feel like the Farmers Insurance commercials that depict a pick-up truck sinking through the ice on a lake, or the deer in the swimming pool, and the patio fire started by an out of control charcoal grill. The tag line is, "We know a thing or two because we've seen a thing or two."

And so have we! Do not doubt for a moment that I have some anxiety about Emily starting college this fall. It is not that I do not trust her. I trust her absolutely. She is a really smart woman with a strong moral compass. But I know a thing or two, and it is the other people out there I don't trust.

Uncertainty, anxiety, and fear often amount to nothing. We wear ourselves out thinking about all of the dangers in the world and it does not change the fact that Emily will go to college, ice fishers will drill another hole in a frozen lake somewhere, and we'll fire up the bar-b-que many more times to come.

Because we know a thing or two, I doubt we can just hope that anxiety will go away. I don't think we can help it. The challenge is our focus. Do we focus on the fear or do we focus on the strengths and resources we have to see us through every challenge. Yes, I mean every challenge that comes our way, including disease, old age, and death; divorce, retirement, and meeting our household budgets.

I think it is also about "who do you trust." Do you trust that evil will win the day? Or do you trust that God's grace will see you through every conflict and loss? Do you trust the basic goodness that is the foundation of the entire creation? It is such an important question that we all need to spend some time meditating on the fundamental goodness of our lives, our families and friends, and the creation.

When we are centered on what I call "Original Goodness," we can let go of some of the distress that plagues us. We can open ourselves to the blessings of life and the people we care about. We will even grow in courage to meet the world on its own terms and move graciously through it.

Be centered and know that I am here for you. *Gary*

The Chaplain's Chart – for the Week of April 17, 2017

A colleague of mine posted on Facebook yesterday that he could not believe he was back in his church office the day after Easter. Nearly every minister who replied scolded him for not taking care of himself. There was one exception who stated that "the work of ministry is never done." What utter nonsense. I know many clergy who take the whole week off after Easter.

Holy Week always wears me out. Aside from the normal tasks of ministry and chaplaincy, I participated in four Good Friday services between our hospital and Hesston. I prepared for Resurrection Sunday. That service included the dedication of a newborn, sermon, and Holy Communion. We had a huge Easter dinner at our house Sunday evening. In the midst of all of this I heard three different stories of people who had seen "ghosts" or had the experience of what psychologists call "sensed presence."

All of us who work with people can get worn down, not just by the physical demands but the emotional ones as well. In fact, I would rather go to bed at night having worked a full day on our little farm than try to go to bed after working with people in crisis or despair. I sleep better physically fatigued than when I am emotionally and spiritually depleted.

We simply have to get away and restore our souls. That means taking time to process what we have experienced, breathe fresh air, walk, pray and meditate. It means saying "no" to every demand that is presented as if it was a life and death concern. Unless there is blood – lots of blood – it usually is not.

If you are an introvert like me, you know how essential it is to be alone on a pretty regular basis. I can tell when I have been overcrowded with people and their expectations. I get moody, cranky, and say very unpleasant things. My kids will say, "Dad, take a walk!" I have to get all of those voices, needs, demands, and psychobabble out of my mind. When I can do that, when I can empty myself, room is given for grace to enter in and I can recenter. I get re-oriented, down to the core of my being. I have learned the hard way that when my life is preoccupied by the needs, pains, and hurts of others I can be of no real service to them. Only when I am resting on the lotus of God's love can I truly serve them.

So, what about you? How many hours of PTO have you stacked up? Don't tell me that you might need them for an emergency or sickness. If you don't take time off you will get sick. You will have an emergency. You earned the time and I want to encourage you to plan a well-earned time off. Don't go down Guilt River and say, "But if I take a week off it will put a burden on the other people in my department." Nonsense! If they are smart they will do the same thing.

And by the way, YOU ARE WORTH TAKING CARE OF.

Gee, I'm getting kind a crabby writing this. I'd better go take a walk. Until I get back, don't forget that I am here for you!!!
Chaplain Gary Blaine

The Chaplain's Chart – for the Week of May 29, 2017

I knew a man who had chest pain for several days. In fact, EMS was called to his house. It was determined that the man was in cardiac arrest and should be taken to the hospital. But the man refused. He said he was afraid that if he went to the hospital he would never return home. Two days later he was dead. He was at home, but dead – dead – dead!

Or consider the man who was diagnosed with end stage lung cancer. I called on him several times in the hope that we could discuss the quality of life that he might yet still enjoy. I was thinking of how he would say goodbye to his wife, children, and grandchildren. Perhaps his death would be a meaningful one. Memorial planning would help create the kind of service that would faithfully represent his values and convictions. Sadly, he was in absolute denial about his disease and would not talk with anyone about any of these concerns.

I have witnessed women and men engage their diseases and even their deaths with courage and some in absolute terror. Some were devout Christians or members of some other religious tradition. Some were not. Quite frankly, I cannot always tell whether faith is a true strength in the face of disease or death. Sometimes it seems so. Other times it seems not. Piety is no assurance of courage when life's tragedies strike us with all their fury.

Where does true courage come from? Mark Twain wrote, "Courage is resistance to fear, mastery of fear – but not the absence of fear." No matter what you believe, fear is a reality of life.

May I suggest that courage grows as we face our fears? Courage matures as we resist fear, even against all odds. The biggest step in mastering fear is facing it.

A parishioner came to see me because she was waking up in the middle of the night weeping. Cheryl was a very busy mother of two young daughters, worked as a librarian full time, and was completing her master's degree in library science. She got up in the morning to get her kids ready for school; went to work; returned home to prepare dinner and help with homework; and then did her own class work. After some prodding and poking I learned that Cheryl had been diagnosed with a rare and potentially fatal liver disease. Cheryl never talked about it, even with her husband. She imagined that if she kept very busy she would not have to deal with it. Because she had not allowed time for her fear and anxiety it woke her up in the middle of the night for release and expression. For the next several weeks we worked on naming the disease, understanding its possible outcomes, how she might manage her disease, especially if it proved fatal. In other words, Cheryl turned her face into the storm and faced her fear. From there her courage grew.

Every seaman knows you have to tack into the storm if you ever hope to ride it out. That is harder than is sounds because there is a brief period of time when your boat or ship is broadside to the storm and you can be easily capsized. But if you try to sail with the storm it will overwhelm your craft and possibly push you into reefs or rocky shores.

I do not know a single human being who does not struggle with major life issues and the accompanying fears. I do not always know what they are, but I know they are there. Whatever you are trying to deal with turn your face toward the challenge and be prepared for courage.

And by the way, you do not have to do it alone. I am here for you.

Chaplain Gary Blaine

174

The Chaplain's Chart – for the Week of July 3, 2017

On my way home from picking up my son, Christopher, for his wedding last weekend I heard a "tap, tap, tapping" sound. He did not hear it. Then I smelled oil. By the time we got home the tapping became clanking. I had thrown a rod. I am not complaining. I had over 280,000 miles on it. Our trusted mechanic of over ten years looked at it, and checked on used or rebuilt engines. Josh told us that the cost would come out to about $5,000 and he did not recommend it.

So, we spent the next few days on the internet looking for possible replacements. We left on Saturday morning with a few good leads. By 5:00 I was on my way home in a 2010 Chevrolet Silverado with a towing package and four wheel drive. Despite its age, it has only 35,000 miles on it, and it is immaculate. I wish you could have seen Mimi in action.

The finance manager came out to talk with us. The suggested retail price was $20,000, which they had lowered to $18,000. "Can you do better than that?" asked Mimi.

"What do you want?" asked the manager.

"I need a step bar and mud-flaps," I said.

"And can you come down another $1,000?" asked Mimi.

The manager look a little stunned and said, "I can't do all of that!" So he went back to the office. When he came back he offered to throw in the step bar and the mud-flaps, and take $500.00 off the price.

"What kind of interest rate are you charging?" Mimi persisted. He said something like 4.5%.

"Well," answered Mimi, "My son is a manager at First Bank in Newton and he can offer 4.25%."

The manager went back to his office. By this time he was breaking a sweat. And when he came back the offer was 4.0%.

What also makes this deal such a good one is the fact that it comes with a lifetime warranty on the powertrain. So even if I throw a rod in the Silverado I am covered.

Is this a story of good luck/bad luck, or God's punishment/ God's grace? No. It is a story of ordinary people dealing with ordinary experiences. Everywhere someone's car is breaking down, or their air conditioner went out, or the school called to say their child has been suspended. It is a story of doing your homework and bargaining with an automobile company that is willing to work with you and still make their own profit. Sometimes we want to make something bigger than it is or add on layers of meaning that are just not there. Life happens and you do the best you can. Sometimes things work out for the good, but not always. That does not mean that some people have super powers and others are just ill-fated.

So be of good cheer. You have everything inside of you to live a good life, even when you throw a rod in your car or truck.

I am here for you.

Gary

The Chaplain's Chart – for the Week of July 17, 2017

On Saturday evening Mimi and I put our kayaks in at Sand Creek. It is a lazy paddle that was, nonetheless, relaxing and enjoyable. There were plenty of beautiful sights, including ducks with ducklings in tow, huge frogs, and a beaver. My favorite was the Mississippi Kites that soared above.

Mississippi Kites are associated with the Mississippi basin, but they have been moving to the southwest with the expansion of new growth trees and hedgerows. Tall trees are their favorite perching and nesting places. They nest in colonies and usually travel in pairs but it is not uncommon to see groups of eight or ten at a time. I can find them consistently over Bethel College and have seen them regularly just west of the hospital.

Mississippi Kites are very sleek and it is a joy to watch their aerial acrobatics. They are small predatory raptors, eating insects, frogs, toads, snakes, small rodents, and birds. The female lays one to two eggs, with an incubation period of about 30 days. The chicks are ready to fly after five weeks. Kites migrate as far south as Argentina in the winter.

After an hour of paddling we loaded up the kayaks and headed home. It was dark by this time. I had a solid night's sleep.

You may not find any of this interesting, and that is fine. I hope, however, that you will not neglect the importance of nature to the healing and nurturing of the human soul. Since the 1980's the Japanese have developed research on the mindfulness practice *shinrin-yoku*, which means "taking in the forest atmosphere." The common term is "forest bathing." Their research has shown that forest bathing reduces blood pressure and stress hormones.

Forest bathing is a wonderful blend of mindfulness and nature. It is the practice of being aware of the forest environment, our original home as human beings. That means we stop to pay attention to the songs of birds, wind blowing, bees humming, and water falling. We breathe deeply the aroma of pine trees, flowers, and the humus of earth and leaves. Pay attention to the colors of leaves, birds, animals, and sun. Feel the texture of leaves, flowers, bark, stones, and sand. If you return to the same place over a year all of these will change. Forest bathing means to be to present to and absorbed by nature. Our self-differentiated, ego focused, and neurotic identities get lost in the wonder and power of the environment. We become one with the creation.

Not surprising that many of the famous Buddhist masters were found in forests, on mountains, or beside rivers and waterfalls.

I am always reminded that human being's first encounter with the Creator occurred in the garden, or forest, or woodlot. In my faith, nature remains the primal connection that I have with God. I invite you to step into the world of nature; step out of yourself; bathe yourself in the pools of creation. I know that for me, time spent with Mississippi Kites better prepares me for a week of hospital chaplaincy than just about anything else I do. As Thoreau wrote, "Nature spontaneously keeps us well. Do not resist her."

Come walk – or paddle – with me.
Chaplain Gary Blaine

The Chaplain's Chart – for the Week of August 28, 2017

On Saturday Mimi and I went grocery shopping, starting with the Farmer's Market in Newton. There we got corn, cantaloupe, and watermelon. We have gotten consistently good melons there all summer long. We also slipped over to Walmart to pick up more guavas to make jelly with. At Dillon's I stocked up on blueberries. Saturday afternoon I put up 8 pints of blueberry preserves. I will start on the guava tonight.

In his essay, "Huckleberries," Henry David Thoreau wrote, "Diet-drinks, cordials, wines of all kinds and qualities, are bottled up in the skins of countless berries for their (human's) refreshment, and they quaff them at every turn." I still need to preserve peaches, pears, strawberries, and raspberries. Our larder should then be ready for the winter.

Sunday evening we had 13 guests over for our "Thanksgiving in August." We served turkey, stuffing, mashed potatoes, gravy, sweet potato soufflé, and a variety of fruits, salads, and desserts. I think we will make it an annual affair. Our guests observed that the traffic was very light for a Thanksgiving Day.

The ages of our guests ranged from four to eighty. There were lots of stories told and a grand canyon of jokes and laughter. Friends and neighbors shared their hopes and plans for the future. One dear friend revealed she has stage three breast cancer. But in that moment the love and joy around the table conquered disease and death. Even though I went to bed exhausted it was the most redemptive Sunday service I have attended in many years.

No one would claim our repast as elegant or gourmet dining. Nor is there any pretense about the social status of our guests. Common and simple food for ordinary callers. Each has a story to tell, a burden uniquely their own, and a sense of humor we did not quite anticipate.

There are a few words for all of this, such as providence and grace. We did not sing the "Doxology" or recite the "Apostle's Creed." But all were fed with abundance and each was strengthened for the week ahead. I don't think church, and certainly not religion, is any more profound than our Thanksgiving in August.

It is like a little diner in Columbus, Ohio, "Nancy's Kitchen." Chicken gravy over mashed potatoes, fried chicken, corn, dinner rolls, and a piece of fruit pie, all for $3.00. A long winding counter is for college kids, judges, carpenters, cops, priests, and bag ladies. Everybody is welcomed. And next to the cash register is a huge pickle jar filled with cash for the high school boy who dove into the shallow end of the pool and broke his neck, or the young woman dying of AIDS, or the family whose house blew up because their gas line had a leak in it.

I think this is what Jesus was talking about when he told stories about the eternal banquet or the woman who hid the leaven in the dough, or when he fed the 5,000. If you cannot find that table, please call me. Come to Soggy Bottom and we will break bread together.

Chaplain Gary Blaine

The Chaplain's Chart – for the Week of September 5, 2017

We sometimes have the wrong impression that chaplaincy or pastoral care is some kind of magic or even necromancy. Ministry has become so professionalized as to become sterilized. People think that chaplains conjure up some special prayer or ritual that brings divine intervention that cures everything from cancer to diabetes. It is imagined that clergy alone can do these things.

I am pleased to tell you that is utter nonsense. The essence of chaplaincy and pastoral care is to bear the burdens of our fellow human beings. We carry them for a little while, for as long as we can, with as much strength as we can muster. Especially for hospital chaplains, it may be only for a little while and a short distance as well. We hope we can get them safely through the emergent need and hospitalization. And then we must release them back to the primary care physician, home health, hospice, family, and faith community. Other spiritual guides will walk with them a little further down the road.

But what does it mean to carry their burden? Fundamentally it means to hear their story, hold their fears, wipe their tears, tickle their funny bone, and invite the Holy Spirit of God's peace into their souls. It does not mean that we answer impossible questions like, "Why did God let this happen?" Or, "Why doesn't God take him or her?" And my favorite, "What did I do to deserve this?" Well probably a lot, but that is a moot question now.

To bear the burden of others means to sit with them, even through long periods of silence. The ministry is being present to them, not solving ridiculous metaphysical riddles. You can even say, "I do not have an answer for your question. What I do know is that I am here for you. God is with us. You are not alone. We will not leave you." The greatest fear of the dying is dying alone, not the absence of a theologian in their death chamber.

As I said before, this is something that you can do. It is not easy, carrying the burdens of others. But in the end it humanizes the world and ourselves. It is often hard and perplexing. It will often leave you wondering if you met their needs. And such ministry is never over. This past weekend I talked with a parishioner who has breast cancer. I wrote a letter to an attorney on behalf of two children whose father constantly interjects anxiety into their lives and is now demanding more visitation privileges. I tried to give encouragement to a friend in Houston. Every day I hold in my heart the fragile health of my dear friend and editor. Throughout the week I could hear from parishioners and friends across the United States who are hoping for a better outcome for their lives, or who are grieving the death of a loved one, or who are shocked to find out they are old. And all of this on top of my responsibilities at the hospital. But that is not complaint. This is the life I have chosen and this is the life I love. All of it galvanizes my humanity as God pounds me on the anvil of mercy, fashioning me to the greater purposes of grace.

There is not a single person who reads this that is not able to bear the burdens of others. Take them as far as you can and as far as they will allow you.

I am here for you!
Chaplain Gary Blaine

The Chaplain's Chart – for the Week of September 18, 2017

Yesterday my stepson, Wes, and his friend, Dalton, came out to our house to dig a couple of fence posts. We are replacing some fencing that is ten years old and some of the posts are rotting. We don't have a power augur, so they were stuck with the post-hole digger and shovels. The first couple of inches were easy enough, but then they went through layers of clay and rock. It did not help that the soil was bone dry and did not have the softness that rain would have produced. But they got through it and maybe today's rain will help settle the posts.

I think our spiritual lives are very much like digging postholes. The first three or four inches are fairly easy. But a few inches would not hold up a five inch by eight foot post. We like to sink ours at 36 inches. There were times when Wes and Dalton made good progress but then they would strike a vein of hard clay. They would pound the posthole digger down into the hole, pull the handles apart, bring the tool up to the top and open the spades, only to watch a teaspoon of dirt drop onto the mound of earth. They used a crowbar to pick and pry at the stony clay obstruction. It was slow going and hard work. But in the end the post should last us ten years and keep a lot of animals where they ought to be.

Spiritual growth is a lot like digging postholes. If you conscientiously work with God to develop your soul you will encounter obstacles and tough going. Perhaps it is more accurate to say that if you are willing to let God work with your soul. This work is done in long hours of prayer, meditation, contemplation, scripture, and deep silence. It is best done in communities of disciplined practice with a spiritual director. There are moments of feeling deeply centered, at peace in the love and joy of God. But there will always be hard places that seem as if your relationship with God is stale, boring, and stuck. In some cases it is as if God is absent. After her death, the private papers of Mother Theresa of Calcutta revealed that for the last fifty years of her life – and despite a daily discipline of prayer – she did not feel the presence of God.

People like St. John of the Cross called this experience the "dark night" (of the soul). Some describe the entry into the dark night as the sense of being stranded. As the dark night falls ever deeper you don't know where you are spiritually. In these very depths of the dark night you come to the realization that there is nothing that can save you, including all of your possessions, your friends, your church, your education, your wealth, or your work. You enter what some identify as "sovereign solitude." You have tried everything and you are ultimately alone. The path out of the dark night is acceptance, or if you will, surrender to this solitude.

You might have to live a while in that solitude. And it is there that God moves like the fresh breezes of the Gulf of Mexico. The sails of our souls flutter and then flap and finally fill the main with God's presence.

Some people will experience the dark night once in their lives or several times. As we have seen with Mother Theresa, some never seem to return. I also think it is important to understand that the dark night is not depression. Those who have experienced the dark night are able to continue their work, family and social life just fine. Their dark night does not lead them to suicide or drug abuse. While they go about their activities of daily living they are aware of an emptiness in their souls. Not everyone agrees with me on this and associates the dark night with something like depression. It is a profound sense of loss but not to the extent that we become dysfunctional. I describe my experience with the dark night with a spiritual dryness, like an old cork in a wine bottle that crumbles apart with every twist of the corkscrew. Nasty little bits fall into wine fouling the drinking of it.

Life events like divorce, disease, unemployment, or the birth of a child do effect our souls. The spiritual dynamics shift and sometimes knock us off balance. But more often than not we enter the dark night when we have become content and complacent or lazy. We enter the dark night when God decides we need a "make over." And it is God who will lead us out one day. And we will be utterly transformed.

Chaplain Gary Blaine

182

The Very Hand of God

Keri is a young nurse with only one year of experience. She is bright, eager, and hardworking. A few days ago a woman presented to the ER with stomach cramps. We discovered that she was 22 weeks pregnant. She did not know that, in part, because she had not had a menstrual cycle in two years. She reappeared Sunday with a painful pressure in her pelvic floor. Keri was processing her through triage. The woman said that she needed to use the bathroom.

Keri directed her to the bathroom, and decided to follow her, watching for any kind of discharge. Rounding the corner Keri saw a red mass on the floor. The woman was standing next to it. The gestational sac had been expelled and slithered down her thigh. The fetus was moving inside it. The umbilical cord was still attached to the mother. Keri scooped it up and called for help.

The gestational sac was placed on a gurney in the trauma bay. The ER doctor opened it and Keri took a turn doing two finger pediatric compressions. The umbilical cord was tied off and cut. The pediatric oxygen mask covered the baby's entire head. "I could tell it wasn't doing any good," Keri told me. Heart compressions continued for twenty minutes before the doctor pronounced the baby dead.

Despite the fact that Keri knows a 22-week-old fetus is not viable in such circumstances, she felt impotent to alter the course of biology. She now feels guilty because she had never seen such a thing and she was not sure what to do. She had no requisite skills. Keri has seen death as an ER nurse. We talked about the fact that most of the dead she had known were elderly people. It is to be expected. But the death of a 22-week-old fetus was not expected. It was not on the horizon of her experience or even in her imagination. Now it is irrepressibly burned into her memory.

We went through my "clinical" checklist of things for her to be looking for: sleep problems, headaches, backaches, constipation or diarrhea, the usual suspects. We talked about long walks, yoga, water, and more conversation. The whole process is called a debriefing.

One of the most vivid images that Keri shared with me was the fact that after the fetus was placed on the gurney and the doctor was working on it, Keri stood beside the mother who was sitting in a chair. Keri said, "All I could think to do was put my arm around her shoulder and hug her."

I replied, "That was probably the most important thing anybody did in that trauma bay, Keri."

Several days later I asked Keri to show me the hand that she had placed on the mother's shoulder. She showed me her left hand. I took it in my own and peered intently at it. "The very hand of God," I said.

Keri pulled her left hand back and hid it in her right hand. "No way," she insisted.

"Yes, Keri," I replied, "the very hand of God."

finis

EPILOGUE

Gary Blaine worked as chaplain at Susan B. Allen Memorial Hospital for six years beginning in May of 2012. He sent out his first 'Chaplain's Chart' via hospital-wide email on June 11th that year, and continued this practice every Monday from then on. The staff came to look forward to his meditations that were affirming, supportive, and inspirational – a nice break in the midst of the daily grind of work and refreshing way to start off another work week. Eventually he expanded his inspirational emails to include a daily morning 'Grace Note' every Tuesday through Friday – a brief quote, scripture, line of hymn lyrics or poetry to start off the day. Gary's presence was not just appreciated through his emails, but also through his physical presence throughout the hospital and ancillary departments. In addition to visiting with patients and families, he was involved in discharge planning, the palliative care team, medical ethics committee, and emergency management committee. He responded to traumas, code blues, and patient deaths in the emergency department and elsewhere. And most days Gary could be found in the cafeteria during the lunch hour dining with employees and doctors. He also paid close attention to the hospital's weekly employee newsletter and took the time to send birthday cards with handwritten notes to every employee throughout the year via the interoffice mail service. The last year or so, Gary made rounds to every part of the hospital each Friday, pushing a serving cart and delivering a variety of snacks and beverages to staff as they worked.

Gary very quickly became an 'anchor in the storm' for many employees during times of stress or changes in their work and personal lives. This was especially true in the last couple of years of his employment at SBAMH. During that time, the hospital CEO retired and other changes occurred in the upper administration leading to interim staff and changes in management styles which had ripple effects to every department in the hospital. A new CEO was eventually acquired, leading to additional changes. On a much larger scale, significant healthcare reform was taking place at a national level, Medicare and JCAHO requirements were changing and reimbursement rates for services were falling, creating financial difficulties for many healthcare providers. The small El Dorado hospital issued their first hospital-wide layoffs in more than a decade. Among one of the first to be cut was the position of hospital chaplain held by the faithful Dr. Gary Blaine. He was informed of the layoff on the morning of August 14, 2018, asked to pack his things and leave. Although not totally unexpected, it was still a heartbreaking shock to Gary and the many employees who had a deep appreciation of his supportive presence. There was a bit of an outcry by staff, with even a petition presented to the hospital board members to 'get Gary back'. The dust eventually settled, but Gary's absence is still felt today by the staff who continue as faithful servants to the patients of SBAMH.

Upon his termination, one of Gary's first priorities was to hold true to the commitment he had expressed to the hospital employees on a weekly basis for more than six years - "I Am Here For You." Although he could no longer reach out to them at the workplace, he began an email group in which he sent out a weekly meditation and daily grace note to personal email addresses. That quickly blossomed into the creation of his website freshbreadwithgaryblaine.com. His weekly meditations are now published on the site as "Fresh Bread" entries every Monday. Online visitors to the site are able to subscribe for the weekly "Fresh Bread" and daily "Grace Notes" to be delivered to their personal inboxes.

Shari Scheffler, P.T.
Susan B. Allen Memorial Hospital
April 16, 2019

FIRST CHAPLAIN'S CHART

From the Chaplain's Chart – June 11, 2012

I am beginning my third week as your new chaplain. As a new employee of Susan B. Allen Memorial Hospital I have been encouraged to use my "new eyes" to share observations in the quest to be a better service provider.

In fact, I do have a first observation: You are a very welcoming community of medical service providers. Everyone has been very kind to me and most helpful getting me oriented. Thank you for that! Your kindness is evident in your relationships with patients, even when their pain or chronic illness makes them frustrated, or irritable, or just plain difficult to work with. My observation of you is that in profound kindness you offer the best medical skills you know how to deliver, regardless of the prognosis.

You have reminded me that my first task is to be a present kindness to everyone I meet. Some people think that a chaplain's job is to give people faith in the hope that their faith will get them through their current crisis. Of course it does not work that way. My job is to be there for them with compassion and quiet grace. I cannot give them faith but, hopefully, I can elicit from them their own faith and the meaning and purpose that such faith may serve them.

The poet, Longfellow, wrote:

> There is no flock, however watched and tended,
> But one dead lamb is there!
> There is no fireside, howsoe'er defended,
> But has one vacant chair.

That is the reality of our lives, and certainly a reality in the hospital. We cannot change such reality, but we can determine how we will engage the mighty struggle of life and death. I have seen in you the capacity to carefully tend the flock and keep the fires of life stoked with great humility and care, even in the midst of suffering and death.

In my experience that is the depth of a living faith, regardless of the church or denomination you might belong to.

I am here to serve you and hope that you will use me in the tending of those souls who look to us for wholeness.

Yours in faith,

Chaplain Gary Blaine

ABOUT THE AUTHOR

A Biographical Sketch of Dr. Gary Blaine

Gary Blaine grew up in the waters of the Gulf of Mexico. He calls the Gulf the wellspring of his soul. He has also been nourished in the deciduous forests of the Eastern United States, having camped and tramped parts of the Appalachian Trail, immersing himself in her woods, rivers, and streams. Gary now lives on the plains of Kansas.

A graduate of Florida Southern College (B.A. – History) and the Candler School of Theology at Emory University (M.Div. and D.Min.), Gary has done postgraduate studies in English literature. In ministry since 1975, he has served rural, urban, and suburban congregations, as well as hospitals and social service agencies. A published writer and columnist, his work has appeared in The Ohio Observer, the Tulsa World, the Toledo Blade, the Butler Times-Gazette, and the Kansas City Star.

Gary is married to Mimi Leo and their blended family includes six children, the youngest of whom is a student at Wichita State University. They live at "Soggy Bottom," a five-acre plot of land where they care for horses, donkeys, goats, and chickens. Reading and writing are his passion, and he also loves photography and fly fishing.

Photo by Mary Griffin Sparks

You can contact Chaplain Blaine at garyblaine48@gmail.com
He is available for retreats, conferences, and forums to share his
experience in chaplaincy, organic spirituality, and care of ministers.
His website is freshbreadwithgaryblaine.com

An Organic Spirituality

32531

5498-62151FF

CPSIA information can be obtained
at www.ICGtesting.com
Printed in the USA
FFHW012253241119
56089380-62151FF

9 781733 156400